WORLD MISSIONS TODAY

by

Terry C. Hulbert, Th.M., Th.D.
Dean, Columbia Graduate School of Bible & Missions
Columbia, South Carolina

Evangelical Teacher Training Association
110 Bridge Street • Box 327
Wheaton, Illinois 60189

61408

Courses in the Advanced Certificate Program

Your Bible
The Triune God
Biblical Beliefs
Evangelize Thru Christian Education
World Missions Today
Church Educational Ministries or Vacation Bible School!

1 2 3 4 5 6 7 / 4 3 2 1 0 9 8 7 6
Third Edition, 1986

Library of Congress catalog card number: 78-68233
ISBN 0-910566-16-X
© 1979 by Evangelical Teacher Training Association
Printed in U.S.A.

Unless otherwise noted, Scripture quotations are from the New American Standard Bible, ©The Lockman Foundation 1960, 1962, 1963, 1968, 1971, 1972, 1973, 1975, and are used by permission. Other quotations are from the King James Version (KJV); and the New International Version (NIV), ©1973, The New York Bible Society International.

Quotes from *Let the Earth Hear His Voice* ©1975 by World Wide Publications used by permission.

Quotes from Stephen Neill: *A History of Christian Missions* (The Pelican History of the Church, vol. 6, 1964), ©1964 by Stephen Neill. Reprinted by permission of Penguin Books Ltd.

Contents

Foreword

Missions is a thrilling subject! This is because it is God's work and involves many people in many places. God uses people around the world in a program of missions as He accomplishes His purpose of man's redemption. It is difficult to comprehend the magnitude of witness generated by that vast host of believers who spend so much of their adult lives spreading the gospel in obedience to Christ's command.

Missionaries for years have gone forth from their home churches to proclaim the message of Christ to those who need to hear of the hope God offers through His Son. While today's missionary task has changed, the underlying purpose of missions remains the same.

A knowledge of the place of missions in God's program, its history through the years, and the working of God today will challenge you in a wonderful way. While every believer's life will be enriched by this knowledge, Sunday school teachers and church leaders will especially benefit from the evidence and awareness of God at work through His people.

As you read this book, remember God is at work through missions. One purpose of the book is to provide an overview of missions so you will pray for, work for, and give to missions and inspire others to similar interest. Another purpose is to acquaint you with mission trends today. A glossary is included at the end of the text to familiarize you with current missions terminology.

I encourage each church teacher and leader to more than simply read this book. While just reading it will be a challenge, a study of this text should result in acting out its message of mission involvement. The book contains numerous suggestions for the advancement of mission interest in the local church. These could well transform a disinterested group into a vibrant, active, praying, and sending church.

E.T.T.A. considers a study of missions so essential to good teacher preparation that *World Missions Today* is a required course in the Advanced Teachers Certificate Program of the Association. Every church might profitably present it as a course of leadership preparation for any of its ministries.

Paul E. Loth, Ed.D., *President*
Evangelical Teacher Training Association

1

Motivation for Mission Involvement

A Nigerian boy hears that Jesus died for him. Despite much persecution, he holds fast to his faith and eventually earns a doctorate at a large North American seminary.

A farmer in a Colombian village turns from a formalized religion when he learns of the possibility of a personal relationship with Jesus Christ. He begins studying the Bible to learn how he can minister to the needs of his people in this poverty-stricken, strife-torn country.

What do these two men have in common? Missionaries brought the gospel to both the Nigerian boy and the Colombian farmer; they believed it and acted upon their faith. Later Nigerian Byang Kato led a continent-wide association of evangelicals, participated in a world congress on evangelism, and promoted biblical Christianity in Africa. As a result of Scripture study, Colombian farmer Gregorio Landero recognized his responsibility to reach out and meet the material needs of his people. He recruited competent teachers of farming and marketing methods to train the people. Such Christian initiative resulted not only in a higher standard of living; but also in many receiving the Savior.

Kato and Landero are but two men whose lives have been transformed by the gospel. They, in turn, were able to win many of their countrymen to Christ because missionaries had crossed cultural, religious, and economic barriers to communicate the news of Jesus Christ to them. When the great multitude, which no one will be able to count, from every nation and tribe and tongue stands before the throne, case histories like these will be told by the tens of thousands.

World missions has developed dramatically in recent years. In our generation, as never before, whole areas of the world and groups of people have become open to the gospel. More Christians have gone more places, learned more languages, translated more Scripture, and established more churches than in any other period of history. In almost every non-Muslim, non-Communist country, Christians are joining this outreach. They are recognizing missions as a central purpose in Christ's church.

Scope of mission involvement

Missions is not limited to activities done by a few overseas, but is a whole process in which all believers can and should be actively engaged. Missions involves establishing a relationship with lost people so the gospel can be demonstrated and communicated in a way they understand. Those who believe the good news are discipled and joined together as a community of believers—the body of Christ. This basic biblical task is to be carried on in all parts of the world.

While fear of the unknown and the vastness of the task may tend to dim a vision for foreign missions, the Lord emphasized the need to reach out to all nations, even the remotest parts of the earth. The Apostle Paul followed these directives and concerned himself with preaching the gospel in the regions beyond.

While we recognize that evangelizing the people in one's own country is important, this book is concerned primarily with communicating the gospel across cultures to meet needs of the over 3 billion people who have no one to tell them of Jesus Christ. This requires specially trained personnel totally committed to Jesus Christ and willing to live in different, sometimes antagonistic, cultural settings. Missionaries must be selected and sent by the Lord of the harvest. Support, prayer, and encouragement must come from the church of Jesus Christ.

Reasons for mission involvement

Why missions? Recognition of man's need for salvation, human compassion, and desire to change world conditions are frequent responses. While these are valid replies, they neglect the primary reasons for missions. Scripture shows us that missions is grounded in God's character, Christ's commands, and the condition of the lost who have never heard the gospel.

God's character

God is holy and hates sin. He created eternal punishment for Satan and his rebellious angels, but does not want any one to perish with them. God loves the people He created from dust and has provided a means of restoring them to fellowship with Himself. He has made salvation available through Jesus Christ. Unless people hear and believe the gospel, they will receive God's judgment. As a holy God, He cannot accept sinners until they have been redeemed. Missions, therefore, is based on both God's holiness and His love.

Christ's command

With authority and unmistakable clarity, Jesus involved every believer in missions. This does not mean that He commanded all to be missionaries, but He did instruct the twelve as well as the larger group of disciples gathered in the Upper Room that they should be involved in discipling all nations. Just as His directives concerning the Lord's Supper extended beyond those present that Passover eve, so the resurrection night command has universal application. Obedience is not optional; Jesus reminded His disciples, "If you love Me, you will keep My commandments."

Condition of the lost

In Luke 16:23-28, the rich man in Hades cried out for mercy and asked that Lazarus the beggar be sent with a drop of water to cool his tongue. When he was told it was too late, he begged that someone be sent to warn his five brothers. Perhaps no more eloquent appeal for missions has ever been uttered. The inexpressible horror of final, eternal separation from God constitutes a compelling reason for missions. The lost not only miss the joy of the Christian life in this world, they must face the inevitable sorrow of judgment for their sins in the next. Without missions those who sit in darkness have no opportunity of coming to the light, no alternative. Considering the present and eternal condition of unregenerate men, missions is essential and urgent.

Results of mission involvement[1]

Active commitment to missions is often a thermometer of a church's spiritual temperature. A church vitally involved in missions is distinct from one which shows little concern for the unreached. Even in New Testament days, a sharp contrast could be seen between mission-minded churches and those which were not. The believers at Corinth, for instance, demonstrated their self-centeredness in destructive interpersonal relationships and in the absence of any apparent concern for the lost. The Antioch church, on the other hand, seriously studied the Word, sent famine relief to their brothers and sisters in Jerusalem, and commissioned Barnabas and Paul for a cross-cultural ministry.

Demonstrates church beliefs

Most evangelical churches have biblically sound statements of doctrine dealing with the authority of Scripture, the hopeless condition of the lost, and the necessity of faith in Christ for salvation. A strong missions program provides tangible evidence that the congregation, when determining priorities, takes its doctrinal standards seriously and seeks to apply them.

Provides resources for worldwide evangelism

The number of potential contacts for Christ and the amount of help provided is directly dependent on the financial resources available. A church which plans and sacrifices to invest heavily in missions significantly affects the scope of the gospel's impact.

Purifies values of believers

Individual Christians who seek God's kingdom first and establish their priorities in accordance with eternal values are more loving, more joyful, and more pleasing to God than those who are self-centered. A mission-involved church tends to encourage its members to make their families, their possessions, and their time available to God. Shared concern for the unreached draws believers together in prayer, giving, and action. Obedience to God and joining with Him in His work around the world produces joy and satisfaction.

Increases local evangelistic concern

The pastor and other leaders must guide the church in balancing its outreach in the neighborhood with its missionary involvement in distant lands. Such a dual thrust has the added advantage of providing in-church training of evangelists, church planters, and Bible teachers for cross-cultural ministry.

Means of mission involvement

World population statistics and a realization of the vast number of individuals who have never heard the gospel easily can discourage well-intentioned Christians. Because we feel we cannot do much, we may be tempted to think that it is pointless for us to try doing anything. We must remember, however, that God knows these statistics. He has the resources available to meet this challenge when His people are willing to be used. Jesus and the disciples demonstrated this principle when feeding 5,000 hungry people. God has commanded us to go to the lost because he desires to save all who will come to Him by faith.

While we may not be able to reach all, we can have a part in reaching some. A concerned Christian may ask: "How can I help? What can I do that will really make a difference?" When we let ourselves be available to God, He has a variety of means ready to involve us in world evangelization. We will consider some of these methods.

Build prayer power

Prayer is undoubtedly the greatest resource in missions. It evidences the concern of individuals and their conviction that only supernatural intervention can accomplish the task of missions. God wants to provide people, resources, and power in answer to our prayers. Jesus said, "Beseech the Lord of the harvest to send out workers into His harvest." Each believer can participate in effectual prayer. The potential for opening closed doors, overcoming opposition, winning large groups of people to Christ, and providing funds is unlimited when backed with prayer power.

Teach missions in the church and family

Most believers are limited in their understanding of the contemporary missions scene. The more believers understand of God's tremendous work in worldwide evangelization today, the more they will want to be involved.

Increase financial investment

God has entrusted His resources to the stewardship of His people. Paul's words to the Corinthians in 2 Corinthians 9:6 still apply: "He who sows sparingly shall also reap sparingly; and he who sows bountifully shall also reap bountifully." Sacrificial giving, wisely directed, is an essential and fruitful means of involvement in missions.

Recruit new missionaries

Much responsibility lies with the local church in recruiting new workers for missionary service. Pastors, parents, Sunday school teachers, and others can be used of God to challenge, instruct, and encourage young adults toward the field of God's calling.

Local churches can have a significant role in strengthening a person in his Christian life, increasing his understanding of spiritual gifts, giving him experience in ministry, and confirming God's leading into missionary service.

Urgency of mission involvement

Each hour thousands of babies are brought into the world and thousands of people leave it. Millions never discover an alternative to the purposelessness and misery of their lives before passing into an eternity of darkness and pain. But for those we can reach with the gospel and who put their trust in the Savior, this life, no matter what its physical wealth or woe, takes on new meaning. Death is no longer an inevitable horror.

The Bible indicates that the person who has never heard about Jesus Christ is lost forever. The key question, however, is not what God will do with the person who has never heard the gospel, but what will He do with those who have experienced salvation and have not responded to His command to share the good news. What does God expect from us? J. Oswald Sanders states, "Our responsibility for the salvation of the heathen will be as great as our ability and opportunity to give them the gospel or to make it possible for the gospel to be brought to them."[2]

Indeed, involvement in world missions is one of the greatest privileges Christ has given His church. Christ's promise "I will build my church" is being fulfilled today. He has given us explicit and unique responsibility in this process.

Summary

Missions is such an important part of church life that each believer should be involved in developing relationships with the lost and then in sharing the gospel with them through verbal and life witness. Reaching the 3 billion people who have never heard of Jesus Christ should be a priority.

The character of God, commands of Christ, and condition of the lost motivate our involvement in missions. Those churches which become active in reaching out to others with the gospel have opportunity to demonstrate doctrinal beliefs, provide resources to further witness around the world, develop God-centered values, and increase local evangelistic concern.

Many types of mission involvement are possible: becoming a missionary, praying, learning about missions, giving money generously, as well as recognizing and developing the gifts of potential missionaries. The time to accomplish these tasks is now. We must make use of the many opportunities and abilities God has given us to bring hope to a dying world.

Notes

Complete bibliographic information for the footnotes at the end of each chapter is given in the Bibliography at the end of the text.

1. The ACMC "How missions-minded is your church?" profile provides a practical instrument for self-evaluation. (See p. 50)
2. J. Oswald Sanders, *How Lost are the Heathen?*, p. 79.

For review

1. What factors are necessary for full development of foreign mission involvement?
2. Name three reasons for mission involvement and explain why each is important.
3. How might a missions-centered church differ from one that is not?
4. In what ways can Christians become involved in missions? How is your church involved?

For additional reading

Griffiths, Michael. *God's Forgetful Pilgrims*. Grand Rapids: Eerdmans, 1975.

Schindler, Marian and Robert. *Mission Possible*. Wheaton, IL: Victor Books, 1984.

Winter, Ralph D. and Hawthorne, Stephen C. *Perspectives on the World Christian Movement*. Pasadena, CA: William Carey Library, 1983.

2

A Biblical Perspective of Missions

Some people regard missions at best as an extension of North American denominations and at worst as the imposition of Western culture. Others view missions as spreading political influence or as a massive welfare program for underdeveloped nations. Still another group equates missions with "civilizing," a carry-over from a colonial concept which assumed Western ways were best. Such impressions of missions are inaccurate and unbiblical.

From a biblical perspective, missions does not originate in human relationships. Instead, missions begins with the divine initiative. God so loved the people He created that, even in their rebellion, He seeks to redeem and restore the lost. Not only does God seek the unsaved, He also directs believing men and women to be involved in communicating the gospel.

Old Testament

The Old Testament introduces God's plan of redemption. As part of His ultimate goal to provide salvation for all people and to communicate the good news of this provision, God revealed Himself to selected men and a separated nation. He also reached out to other nations in a variety of ways. God cared for both Rahab and Ruth and showed concern for "strangers" in the midst of Israel. Jonah was required to enter Gentile territory and preach to the people of Nineveh.

There is a unity and a continuity in all that God does. What He revealed in Old Testament days is consistent with and part of all He has been doing among men in every age. God's revelation of His purposes is progressive. Sacrifices in the Old Testament days brought into focus what God was saying about redemption. The Passover lamb, for instance, foreshadows the "Lamb of God who takes away the sin of the world" and the death of Christ. An understanding of the basic concepts revealed in the Old Testament, therefore, can help us see the plan of God in contemporary missions.

Need of salvation

The human race has degenerated progressively since Adam disobeyed God. History records a world sinking ever deeper into idolatry, sensuality, and depravity. Three times in the first chapter of Romans, Paul used the words "God gave them up" to remind the people that God had relinquished mankind to the consequences of their rebellious choices.

The first eleven chapters of Genesis reveal the origin of sin and the fact that God must judge it. Although sin entered by one man, it was practiced by each of his descendants. Cain was guilty of hatred and murder, Lamech of polygamy and blood revenge, the antediluvians of incest and violence, Noah of intemperance, Ham of lack of respect and modesty, and the Babel builders of rebellion and self-glorification. Even Noah had no merit of his own. He had to find grace in the eyes of the Lord. Because all have sinned, missions is concerned with reaching all men.

God demonstrated His despair over man's sin when he destroyed the human race. The extent of the flood, drowning all but eight who accepted God's provision, reveals that God will indeed judge all sinners. The flood was a historic preview of the ultimate judgment to be placed on all who do not find salvation in Jesus Christ. The final condemnation and its consequences will be as comprehensive as the flood.

Provision of salvation

Throughout the Old Testament, God was preparing a people to witness to the nations concerning His person and provisions, particularly the provision of redemption. Israel was the means through which He would speak, but not the extent of the persons He would save.

At the moment when all men sinned in Adam, God promised a Redeemer who would provide restoration to fellowship with Himself. In His call to Abraham, God made an all-encompassing promise, "and in you all the families of the earth shall be blessed."

A thousand years later, David, in his Psalms, often spoke of a salvation for the Gentiles. When his son Solomon dedicated the Temple as the center of worship of the Lord, he included in its ultimate purpose the witness to all men, "that all the peoples of the earth may know Thy name." Toward the end of the Old Testament period, the prophets frequently referred to salvation for the Gentiles even while denouncing their sins and warning of judgment.

New Testament

Jesus' statement in John 20:21, "As the Father has sent Me, I also send you," summarizes missions in the New Testament. The Gospels record Jesus' obedience in fulfilling the mission on which His Father sent Him. The Acts and the Epistles record the church's response to Christ's Great Commission, especially as reflected in the life and ministry of the Apostle Paul.

The Gospels

When Jesus identified Himself with men to reveal the glory of the Father, He bridged the ultimate cultural gap—the separation between heaven and earth, God and man. This is recorded in John 1:14, "The Word became flesh, and dwelt among us." Jesus was motivated by love for the Father and love for people in their need, not by desire for adventure or self-glorification. Basic mission concepts were present in His birth, life, and death.

Many facets of Jesus' ministry reflect and reinforce the missionary nature of His life. Not only did Jesus reveal Himself as King of the Jews with mighty acts and fulfill many of the prophets' predictions, He also moved with ease among those whom His people despised. He made contact with the Samaritans through His communication with the woman at the well of Sychar. Later, Jesus healed Samaritan lepers and made many fruitful contacts with the Romans, even healing the son of an officer. In addition, He taught and healed in Greek cities and other Gentile areas. Such modeling of cross-cultural communication resulted in many later responding to the preaching of Philip and the apostles.

Jesus revealed His concern for all of mankind when He gave His reason for coming to earth: "To seek and to save that which was lost." His threefold parable in Luke 15 clearly reveals the basic mission concept that God loves sinners, seeks till He finds them, and receives them when they repent. In John 10:16 Jesus referred directly to His desire to save Gentiles: "I have other sheep, which are not of this fold; I must bring them also." His plan for the future was to build His church, a body of believers worldwide.

On the night before the crucifixion, Jesus' ministry in the Upper Room climaxed a candidate school for those who would lead the first missions thrust in history. Almost every verse of John 13—17 reveals the fiber of missions. He stressed the importance of the Holy Spirit, prayer, bearing fruit, dealing with opposition, and going into a hostile world so that many might believe on Him.

In Christ's post-resurrection ministry, the most prominent feature was the Great Commission.[1] Speaking with all authority, He gives the basic command: *as you are going make disciples of all nations.* Obedience to this missionary mandate involves:

- Communicating persuasively the facts of the gospel in a way which has meaning for the hearer. The gospel must penetrate all cultures and all languages, reaching men and women in all parts of the world.
- Leading individuals to accept the finished work of Christ by repenting and believing on Jesus as Lord and Savior.
- Separating converted sinners from self-centered relationships and helping them identify with the body of Christ by establishing them in the loving, Christ-centered community of the church.
- Teaching believers to use their spiritual gifts and live victoriously over sin by the power of the Holy Spirit.

• Instructing and leading believers in effective ministry and witness in their community and, for those selected by the Spirit, into a cross-cultural communication of the gospel.

The Acts and the Epistles

Pentecost marked a turning point in God's reaching out to the lost. Jesus had paid the penalty for sin, conquered the bondage of death, and returned to the presence of the Father. With His work finished, the disciples were commanded to continue all that Jesus had begun and taught. God was implementing a systematic plan to communicate continuously the good news to every corner of the earth until Christ's return.

Jesus' parting promise recorded in Acts 1:8 informed His disciples that their power was to be supplied by the Holy Spirit as they purposed to be His witnesses and planned to establish an ever-widening witness in Jerusalem, Judea, Samaria, and the remotest parts of the earth. Being led away from Jerusalem as far and as fast as possible was a radical concept. Since the days of David, Jerusalem had been the place where men met with God. Now, Christianity had to become mobile and penetrate all cultural settings to introduce people to God. Consequently, the disciples were commanded not to leave Jerusalem until the Spirit came to indwell and empower them. With the Holy Spirit indwelling him, each believer could go out and witness.

The book of Acts records the first thirty years of the church and the fulfillment of Jesus' promise. For the first seven years, the apostles evangelized Jews and proselytes in Jerusalem and the surrounding towns. In spite of internal and external stresses and severe persecution, the church thrived. A committed company of believing, sharing, praying, learning, and witnessing people bound themselves together as the body of Christ. Persecution and spiritual momentum carried these witnesses thirty miles north to the heart of Samaria, the first cross-cultural penetration into an area Jesus Himself had pioneered.

The number of Gentile believers greatly expanded with the conversion of Saul of Tarsus (Paul) and the introduction of the gospel at Caesarea, the governmental center for Palestine. From there, the good news spread some three hundred miles northward to Antioch, the third largest center of the empire. The discipled church at Antioch submitted to the Spirit as He sent out Barnabas, Paul, and John Mark. These men broke new ground, evangelizing Gentiles and Jews of the Dispersion. Within a few years, the area now occupied by Turkey, Greece, and southern Yugoslavia was evangelized and evangelizing. In addition, churches in such key cities as Philippi, Thessalonica, and Ephesus became sending churches like the one at Antioch. The witness which began in Jerusalem, the Jewish religious capital of the world, reached to Rome, the Gentile political capital. Between these two cities, apostles and new believers discipled thousands of people from a variety of cultures.

It is doubtful if Paul or his associates ever consciously developed a mission strategy. We can discern, however, several mission principles in the Spirit's leading and the ability of these ministers of the gospel to meet new situations.

- *Identification with lost men and women.* Rejecting his extreme pharisaical separatism, Paul strove to accept and be accepted by sinners of every social, ethnic, and religious group. He worked to become all things to all men.
- *Involvement with a home church.* Paul maintained close bonds with the church at Antioch and reported back after each missionary journey to these unnamed saints who had confirmed his call and had been instruments of the Holy Spirit in commissioning Barnabas and himself.
- *Concentration on influential cities.* The Holy Spirit directed those sharing the gospel to centers of Roman administration and Greek culture. These were places from which the Word could flow naturally to other centers along commercial, military, governmental, and personal lines of communication. Philippi was a "little Rome;" Athens, the cultural center of Greece; Ephesus, the religious center of the empire; Corinth and Thessalonica, centers of commerce.
- *Limitation of work to four provinces.* The Holy Spirit directed Paul westward toward Rome and prevented him from moving into other areas where he would have had a natural concern. Despite his early residence in Damascus and academic connections in Jerusalem, he did not try to reach these centers or the many other parts of the Roman Empire. Paul's purpose was not to make contacts in all the world but to plant churches in selected areas. By limiting the extent of his outreach, it was possible for him to stay in each place long enough to establish a church.
- *Baptism, instruction, and involvement of believers as soon as possible.* Paul had no concern for church politics. His purpose was to make disciples who would become disciplers.
- *Leadership of a team.* Despite his unusual experience and outstanding gifts, Paul was not jealous of his position or protective of his pride. As a leader, he was first and always a servant. Conscious of his weakness and unworthiness, Paul depended on the Lord to work through him to multiply the impact of all members of his team.

The apostle's life and method of ministry hold many implications for missions today. By studying these precedents and making ourselves available to the same Holy Spirit, we can share the excitement and power experienced by that first missionary generation.

Summary

From the promise of salvation to Adam and Eve to the presence of the redeemed in the new heaven and new earth, all Scripture testifies to a seeking, saving God. The mission mandate for our day is rooted in this eternal purpose and plan.

The motivation and method of missions rest on the person and work of Christ, as recorded in the Gospels, and on the priority of the early church, as stated in the Acts and the Epistles. While the apostles bore much lasting fruit, no doubt they would have rejoiced greatly if they could have anticipated its abundant multiplication in the twentieth century. Our generation, in turn, bears its own heavy mission responsibilities as we approach the end of the age of grace and of missions.

For review

1. How does the Old Testament prepare us for the gospel?
2. In what ways did Jesus provide a model for missionary work?
3. Trace the spread of the gospel from Jerusalem to Rome as recorded in the book of Acts, noting especially how this relates to Acts 1:8.
4. How could Paul's strategy in missions be applied in a practical way today?

Notes

1. David J. Hesselgrave, "Confusion Concerning the Great Commission," *Evangelical Missions Quarterly, Vol. 15, No. 4,* October 1979, p. 197.

For additional reading

Kane, J. Herbert. *Christian Missions in Biblical Perspective.* Grand Rapids: Baker Book House, 1981.

McQuilkin, J. Robertson. *The Great Omission.* Grand Rapids: Baker Book House, 1984.

Peters, George W. *A Biblical Theology of Missions.* Chicago: Moody Press, 1972.

Richardson, Don. *Eternity in Their Hearts.* Ventura, CA: Regal Books, 1981.

3

History of Missions: Pentecost to 1800

Missions has passed through several phases in its historical development. For three centuries following Pentecost, the light of the gospel burned brightly and spread far as Christians believed the resurrection message and lived the resurrection life. But with the legalizing of the church under Constantine and its growing political concerns, the light began to dim.

During the Dark Ages that light almost went out as ceremonial religion tended to suffocate rather than spread the flame. Even the Reformation, with its rediscovery of basic truths, did not spark evangelism. As the Pietists in the seventeenth century began to apply biblical truths personally, however, the flame was fed. Through the exciting days of exploration, revolution, and revival in the eighteenth century, it burned even brighter, lighting the way to the century of missions to follow.

Early period: 30-300

First-generation Christians were mission-minded. Although leaders such as Paul and Barnabas specifically are mentioned in Scripture as full-time, church-supported missionaries, it is evident that virtually every Christian was a witness to Jesus Christ. A great mass of non-professional evangelists moved about the empire sharing the gospel in the course of their work contacts.

Extent of expansion

The German scholar Harnack calculates that there were about thirty thousand Christians in Rome by the year 250. Most authorities estimate that 10 percent of the Roman Empire's fifty million people were Christians by 313. More important than numbers was the character of the Christians. While most were slaves, traders, soldiers, and ordinary people, intellectuals, such as Justin Martyr (c. 100-165), also found the gospel offered what philosophy could not.

By the end of the third century, the gospel had permeated all parts of the empire. Syria, Asia Minor, Egypt, and North Africa as well as such metropolitan centers as Rome and Lyons in southern France were the strongest Christian areas. Village and rural people, however, largely were left untouched. Not only had the church expanded to almost every corner of the Roman Empire, it also penetrated the region of Mesopotamia.

Factors contributing to expansion

Greek conquest of the Near Eastern world 300 years before Christ's birth had made Greek the common tongue of the empire. Therefore, although at times cultural barriers interfered, believers generally could witness to unbelievers anywhere and churches could correspond with each other in a common language. In addition, Roman control of much of the world west of the Euphrates made possible trade and travel on the best road systems in the world without the impediment of national barriers.

Jews of the Dispersion lived in almost every city of the empire and taught about the God of the Old Testament and His standard of righteousness. Evangelistic emphasis was on a convincing personal witness to Jesus Christ as Lord and Savior, the need for conversion, and a complete break with the former lifestyle. The commitment and zeal of believers had a great impact on others. Many Gentiles, disillusioned with their bankrupt philosophy and polytheism, were open to having needs met by the gospel.

Following the year 64, two centuries of heavy persecution also contributed to growth of the church. Men and women dying for their faith had to know what they believed and be convicted of its truth. The assurance of such witnesses attracted many to Christ while threats of persecution tended to keep the church purified.

Believers were noted for their uprightness and unselfishness in a world of moral degradation. Their strong sense of community and expression of mutual love in practical ways provided a dynamic contrast to the decaying Roman society and family life. In such a day when meaning and security were scarce, the love of Christ revealed through His church attracted many who saw Him as their only hope.[1]

Medieval period: 300-1500

Events of the fourth century determined the course of the church for the next twelve hundred years. Emperor Constantine (274-337) legalized Christianity and was baptized just before his death. The relatively pure, persecuted church suddenly became the state church. Political and economic concerns began to outweigh evangelism. The church suddenly emerged from obscurity and disfavor into a position of influence and privilege. Dogmas of the church often were accepted without the radical change of life that follows true conversion and faith became superficial.

As corruption and carnal values became a way of life, the church increased in political importance. Rivalries as well as ignorance of scriptural truth or personal application also became more frequent. The commitment to reach the lost diminished as ceremonialism began replacing reality in the Christian life. Church leaders became increasingly concerned with political and financial advancement while the laity became more and more perfunctory in their worship. The chasm between clergy and laity was ever widening.

In spite of these tendencies, Ulfilas reached out to the Goths (341), Patrick to Ireland (432), and other individuals to the pagan tribes who had taken over western Europe. From the year 500, the church entered a period of conflict with two foes—barbarians who eventually were "Christianized" and faithful followers of Islam out to convert the world.

From the beginnings of Islam in Arabia (622), the church concerned itself with survival against this new threat. Muslims conquered North Africa and extinguished the church there. Jerusalem fell in 638 and Constantinople in 1453. Only the Battle of Tours (Spain) in 732 and the Battle of Vienna in 1529 prevented the conquest of all Europe by Islam. The need for a military defense of Christendom, together with the political emphasis of the church, all but paralyzed missionary activity.[2]

Reformation period: 1500-1800

The Protestant Reformation was the most significant and hopeful event in fifteen hundred years for the church and missions. Its challenge to the abuses of the Roman Catholic church and its rediscovery of the authority of the Bible and the way of salvation precipitated a whole new era.

Delay in missionary development

Perhaps the greatest paradox of this period, however, was that these new-found truths did not affect missions for some two hundred years. The new understanding of salvation by faith alone, the translation and printing of Scriptures for personal study, and the excitement of Reformation churches for new freedom lost their potential impact in ecclesiastical wranglings. Although Protestantism evidenced no evangelistic zeal, from 1500 to 1700 the Roman Catholic church won more converts from paganism than it lost to Protestantism.

Kane lists several factors contributing to this impasse:
- The Reformers taught that the Great Commission applied only to the original apostles who fulfilled it in their day. If later generations were without the gospel, it was their fault and the church should not intervene.
- While the Roman Catholic church was launching a successful counter-reformation, the Lutheran and Reformation churches were fighting among themselves. Their Thirty Years War left Germany in economic and social chaos and the church totally uninvolved in evangelism and missions.

- Protestant Europe was isolated from Asia, Africa, and the New World. The Roman Catholic countries of Spain and Portugal were the great exploring and colonizing powers of the day. The largely Protestant British and Dutch peoples did not enter the international scene until a century after the Reformation.
- Protestant churches had no religious orders committed totally to a cause. Groups such as the Franciscans and Dominicans spread the Catholic faith effectively around the world. [3]

Beginning of missionary development

Modern missions began with the Pietists in central Europe. Just as the Protestant Reformation reacted against the Roman Catholic corruption of doctrine and morals, the Pietists reacted against the barren orthodoxy and formalism of the Reformation churches. Pietism began with Lutheran pastor Philip Spener (1635-1705), who emphasized a personal conversion experience, Bible study, prayer, Spirit-filled living, and missionary zeal. Late in the seventeenth century and early in the eighteenth much of the Pietist activity was centered in Halle, Germany. In 1705, the Danish-Halle Mission sent out their first missionaries to the East Indies.

The second thrust came from the Moravian church. In 1722 Count Zinzendorf gave refuge to those fleeing from Roman Catholic persecution. The Moravian colony on his estate became a center for world missions. In 1732 missionaries were sent out to the Virgin Islands and Greenland. Later, others went to Surinam (Dutch Guiana), West and South Africa, Jamaica, and the Indians of North America. In less than a generation, 226 Moravians entered 10 countries with the gospel.

Scotsman Robert Millar advocated prayer for the conversion of the pagan world. By 1746 this idea so caught on that Jonathan Edwards and other Christians in America got involved in a seven-year "Concert of Prayer" for the spread of the gospel throughout the world. The Pietist movement and the evangelical awakening in England and America helped prepare the church for new worldwide concern.

William Carey's book *An Enquiry into the Obligations of Christians to Use Means for the Conversion of the Heathen,* written in 1792, was a landmark in missions history. It advocated taking initiative in reaching the lost, a revolutionary concept which not all could accept. In fact, Carey's own Baptist church responded to his concern with, "Young man, sit down. When God pleases to convert the heathen, He will do it without your aid or mine." Undaunted, Carey, his family, and two associates set sail in 1793 for India where he served forty years.

The title "Father of Modern Missions" has properly been attributed to Carey. His work and influence were instrumental in establishing many new mission agencies, including the London Missionary Society (1795), the Church Missionary Society (1799), the British and Foreign Bible Society (1810), and the American Bible Society (1816).

In the United States, God used students inspired by Carey to ignite interest in missions just as He had used Carey to kindle the flame in Europe. Samuel J. Mills, sensing a call from God as he was plowing, left his farm in 1806 to enroll in college and prepare for seminary. His life touched that of five other young men who became known as the Society of the Brethren. Often they met in a grove of trees for discussion and prayer. Once they were caught by a sudden thunderstorm and sought refuge in a nearby haystack. There they prayed for the unreached people of the world and resolved to become America's first missionaries. This event, now known as the "Haystack Prayer Meeting," marked the beginning of American involvement in overseas missions.

Adoniram Judson, who had led in forming the Society of Inquiry on the Subject of Missions, joined the Haystack Group. Such earnest concern was shown by Judson and other men for missions worldwide that the American Board of Commissioners for Foreign Missions was established in 1810. Two years later, Judson and several colleagues were ordained to take the gospel to India.

Summary

Christianity was destined to spread. Everywhere "new creations in Christ Jesus" were being made. This supernatural reality resisted the pressure of persecution from without and doctrinal division from within. At times, hostile winds had all but blown out the flame, yet the light burned brighter and shone farther as the centuries passed.

With the exploration of new worlds, the gospel had to bridge more diverse and difficult cultural gaps to meet spiritual needs. As with pioneers like Peter, Thomas, Barnabas, and Paul, those who gave themselves to missions could best rejoice in what God was doing.

Believers in each generation have been responsible for communicating the gospel to those living in their time. Some generations succeeded better than others, but the basic dynamic has always been the same—Holy-Spirit empowered individuals bearing witness to Christ where He was not known. The presence and power of the Spirit were as evident in Spener and Zinzendorf in central Europe, for example, as in Peter and John in central Judea. God also used the committed men of the Haystack Prayer Meeting as He had used the praying believers at Antioch.

Notes

1. Stephen Neill, *A History of Christian Missions,* pp. 25-43.
2. Neill, pp. 44-60.
3. J. Herbert Kane, *Understanding Christian Missions,* pp. 140-141.

For review

1. What key factors accounted for the growth of the church from Pentecost to 300 A.D.? What are some parallel factors in missions today?
2. What did the Pietists teach and practice? How did these principles affect missions?
3. What contributions did William Carey make to missions?
4. Relate how each of the following persons or events contribute to the history of missions: Constantine, Spener, Zinzendorf, Millar, Haystack Prayer Meeting, and Judson.

For additional reading

Kane, J. Herbert. *A Concise History of the Christian World Mission.* Grand Rapids: Baker Book House, 1978.

Latourette, Kenneth S. *A History of Christianity, 2 Vols.* New York: Harper L. Row, 1975.

Neill, Stephen C. *A History of Christian Missions.* Baltimore: Penguin Books, 1964.

Tucker, Ruth A. *From Jerusalem to Irian Jaya.* Grand Rapids: Zondervan Publishing Company, 1983.

4

History of Missions: 1800-World War II

For seventeen centuries worldwide evangelism fulfilled the prediction of Christ and demonstrated that the power evident at Pentecost continued. But this was only the beginning. The spread of the gospel and the growth of the church in the 1800s far surpassed everything which came before.

The nineteenth century

Historian Kenneth Latourette termed the nineteenth century "The Great Century" for missions. It began with the impact of the French Revolution on Europe at the end of the eighteenth century and reached its climax at the Edinburgh Missions Conference in 1910. During this period, Protestant missions expanded at the highest rate since Pentecost. Several international and technological factors combined to make this possible.

Factors contributing to missions development

The close of the French Revolution and subsequent defeat of Napoleon in 1814 opened the way for largely Protestant Britain to explore and colonize freely. As religious wars were ending in Europe, this period of relative *world peace was conducive to world colonization.* Nationalistic concerns and the resulting international rivalries also increased pressure for an outward look.

Development of the steam engine and steamship did more than anything else to open up the world for missions. Hundreds of inventions applying the mechanical power of the steam engine to industry created new demands for raw materials. To find the necessary resources and more markets for the products they produced, the British, Dutch, and French were involved in intensive exploration and colonization.

Britain's stand against slave trade as well as the explorations of Livingstone and Rhodes opened up large sections of Africa for missions. Publication of Livingstone's *Missionary Travels and Researches in South Africa* in 1857 encouraged further investigation and missionary penetration of that continent. Other European countries, such as Holland, established large colonies in Africa. Yet, the progress of the gospel was not limited to Africa. India, a country which had long been resistant to missions, became receptive when they accepted British rule. Also, treaties signed by 1858 permitted European nations to enter China.

While European nations were increasing in their influence and spread of beliefs, *Islam began to decline* after a thousand years of dominating the lands around the Mediterranean. Independence movements in Greece and the Balkan countries as well as the advance of France into North Africa reversed the spread of Islam.

In contrast, the *vision for expansion* which had motivated governments and commercial interests was caught by Christian organizations. Missionaries attempted to move into areas explored by their fellow countrymen and establish churches.

At a time when a new wave of missionaries and prayer were most needed, Englishman John Wesley and followers of the Methodist movement sparked *spiritual revival* in New England. While not all Protestant churches were able or willing to become involved in missions, new mission agencies maintained this heightened momentum.

In the last half of the nineteenth century, the second evangelical awakening in the United States began when laymen felt a great burden to pray individually and corporately for missions. The result: a growing sense of responsibility for evangelism and missions. This revival spread to North Ireland and increased the number of missionary volunteers from both sides of the Atlantic.

Survey of major developments

As political horizons expanded and new interaction developed between countries, the opportunity to share the gospel also increased. Since circumstances varied from one location to the next, we will evaluate them individually.

Far East (China, Japan, Korea)

Hudson Taylor arrived in China from Britain in 1853. More than any other person, he was responsible for penetrating this largest of all ethnic groups with the gospel. In 1865, after many disappointments and serious ill health, Taylor established a faith mission supported solely and directly by prayer and faith. The approach of this interdenominational but theologically conservative mission was new. Involvement of individuals with little formal education was welcomed. Being administered from within China, emphasis was placed on evangelizing the people by identifying with them. The Chinese were encouraged to develop their own church and Christian education leaders. Growth was swift. Within thirty years missionaries from around the world were evangelizing in every province.

The Boxer Uprising of 1900 in China was directed against all foreigners and wiped out 135 Protestant missionaries there. Yet this interruption did not diminish the missions thrust. By 1910, the Protestant missionary force had reached more than fifty-five hundred. However, the spread of the gospel was hindered by many Christian Chinese young people becoming more concerned with nationalistic expressions of Christianity than evangelism.

In the Buddhist country of Korea, a visit by Dr. John L. Nevius from China in 1890 was the turning point for Christian missions. He introduced the "Nevius Method." The major features of his plan included: a self-supporting witness, church organization limited to support by the Korean church, church-appointed and supported full-time leaders, and church buildings constructed with local funds. Bible study and annual periods of intensive instruction were used to prepare believers to witness. From 1894 to 1910, Presbyterian and Methodist churches grew to over thirty thousand members with adherents numbering many thousands more. Then, the Japanese invasion of 1910, which ended the Korean empire and brought persecution to Christians, slowed down church growth.

Although American missionaries entered Japan in 1859, Christianity was prohibited until 1873. Early growth was very slow since Christianity was considered an intellectual position not to be responded to with the heart. Growth finally came, however, when the number of missionaries rose from 145 to 451 in the years 1882 to 1888. At the same time, the number of church members grew from five thousand to over twenty-five thousand. While the number of Christians in Japan has always been few, their influence has been proportionally greater than their numbers.

Southeast Asia

A new field was opened for Protestant missions when the United States drove Spain out of the Philippines in 1898. The young people were discontent with the Roman Catholic church and sought Western education. Consequently, missionaries were welcomed as friends.

From 1902 to 1911, the Christian and Missionary Alliance entered Laos, Vietnam, and Cambodia. In Thailand, missionaries were welcomed but resistance to the idea of conversion made evangelism difficult.

The gospel had its greatest impact in Indonesia. No mission to Muslims ever has seen more converts than the Dutch work there. Also, in the mountain areas, the Bataks, who had been untouched by Islam, began turning to Christ in great numbers after strong initial resistance. Many chiefs of this cannibalistic people responded to the gospel. Church membership grew from 7,500 in 1881 to 103,500 in 1911.

South Pacific

In 1858 John Paton pioneered missions in the New Hebrides Islands. In 1870 the first missionaries arrived in New Guinea, which is now known as Irian Jaya. This second largest island in the world is lined with almost impassable mountain ranges. Consequently, evangelism was slow and difficult among the 500 separate language groups populating the island. In 1871 the martyrdom of John Patteson on Nukapu Island resulted in a new wave of support for missions in that area.

India

Although missionaries Carey and Judson had already begun work in India, it was not until Britain took control in 1858 that the door really opened to evangelism. Good administrators unified the country and brought famine under control. Although Muslims and Hindus appreciated the educational and medical benefits which missionaries brought, they were threatened by the changes in lifestyle that Christianity required. In spite of this, between 1851 and 1901, the Protestant community multiplied itself ten times.

Middle East

A new encounter between Christianity and Islam occurred in the Middle East during the latter half of the nineteenth century. This resulted from Christians increasingly trying to understand the nature and origin of Muslim teachings. Samuel Zwemer, who served for sixty years (1891-1951) in Arabia, undoubtedly had the greatest impact on this area.

Africa

Since the seventh century, people from the Sahara Desert northward have been Muslim. Roman Catholic missionaries followed Portuguese exploration during the fifteenth century, but Protestant missions did not reach sub-Sahara black Africa until about 1800. First touched was Sierra Leone by British Baptists in 1795. American missionaries began work in Liberia in 1833, the year Britain abolished slavery. Other missionaries soon went to Ghana and Nigeria.

The next thrust came as David Livingstone and Robert Moffatt opened up south-central Africa in mid-century. Responding to Livingstone's challenge, students moved into central Africa in 1857. British personnel entered Kenya in 1884. Other groups from the United States followed them into Zaire (Congo) in the last quarter of the century.

Missionaries often arrived with the colonizing powers and worked to care for the spiritual, educational, and medical needs of the people. Colonial governments gave significant help and encouragement to these missionary undertakings. Indeed, response to the gospel in Africa over the past 100 years has been greater than on other continents. The multitude of missionaries sent out and the absence of entrenched religions south of the Sahara, except Animism, help account for this encouraging result.

Latin America (Mexico, Central America, South America, and some islands)

Protestant missions did not enter Latin America until the middle of the nineteenth century nor gain any momentum until about 1870. Between 1810 and 1824, Spain lost its hold on Latin America and left each country an independent republic. The 1822 Monroe Doctrine warned European powers to stay away from the Western Hemisphere. Thus, most mission activity during that century originated in the United States or Canada. Many parts of Christendom did not feel a need to go to Latin America because the Roman Catholic church had been there over 400 years. Although the Edinburgh Missionary Conference of 1910 concluded that Latin America was not a mission field, many theologically conservative American missionaries did go there.

Later developments

The first mission sending agencies were interdenominational. As the missionary thrust developed, denominations began to extend their organizations overseas by establishing their own mission boards.

In the latter part of the nineteenth century, *the faith mission* appeared. China Inland Mission (now Overseas Missionary Fellowship) was established in Britain in 1865. New agencies developed in the United States including the Christian and Missionary Alliance in 1877, the Evangelical Alliance Mission in 1890, and Sudan Interior Mission in 1893. Today, faith missions are responsible for a large part of missionary activity. Churches without denominational affiliations are their primary sources of personnel and funds.

Bible societies have played a key role in the development of missions in the past 150 years. Since missions involves communication of the Word of God, it is essential that as many people as possible have copies of Scripture in their own language. Bible societies have been meeting this need with extraordinary effectiveness. Pioneering in the field were the British and Foreign Bible Society (1804), the National Bible Society of Scotland (1809), the Netherlands Bible Society (1814), and the American Bible Society (1816).

For the most part, missionaries have done the translation work with Bible societies providing technical assistance and supervision. Scripture portions, published without notes or comments, are sold at subsidized prices by local missionaries and nationals.

In the 1880s *students* in increasing numbers began *volunteering for missionary service.* One hundred university and seminary students signed the 1886 Princeton Pledge stating, "I purpose, God willing, to become a foreign missionary." In addition, hundreds of young people sought training for missionary service at newly formed schools like Nyack College (1882), Moody Bible Institute (1886), and Ontario Bible College (1894).

Although William Carey's proposal for a world missionary conference in 1810 had been scorned, 100 years later his dream became a reality. More than 1,350 delegates from 153 mission agencies around the world gathered for the Edinburgh (Scotland) Missionary Conference. Chairman John Mott challenged students to complete the "evangelization of the world in our generation."

The early twentieth century

A number of forces and events affected missions during the twentieth century. These changes led missions in a considerably different direction than previously pursued.

Forces affecting missions

Success in industrialization and colonization created an atmosphere of well-being, of invincibility, and of endless horizons in Western thinking. War was unthinkable. Western civilization was indestructible. As a result of increasing numbers of missionary recruits, Bible conferences, and training institutions, the outlook for missions was optimistic.

World War I, however, shattered this confidence as the colonized and newly "civilized" peoples of the world began to doubt the values of those countries that fought such a war. A new nationalism which resented foreign dominance and sought national identity increased the reaction against the West. Since the missionary had arrived about the same time as the colonial administrator, their images were related. A hard realism was needed to separate missions from its political context. Missionary personnel had to begin adjusting to a new era.

Although at the Edinburgh Conference it was assumed that biblical Christianity had no peer, following the war many began to question the uniqueness of Christianity. Even many theologians were beginning to accept other religions as equal to Christianity. The second world missionary conference at Jerusalem in 1928 clearly reflected this change of thinking.

Events affecting missions

The *Russian Revolution of 1917* set in motion a new anti-Christian force which, in less than half a century, posed the greatest threat to Christianity since the conquest of Islam. While the aspirations and aims of communism seemed reasonable enough at first, they involved theological implications in direct opposition to the gospel.

Economic chaos in America during the 1930s caused a sharp drop in missions recruiting and income. Yet missionaries continued going to the field while churches sacrificed to support them. In fact, one mission board called for and got 200 new recruits during this period.

In 1932 the *Layman's Foreign Mission Inquiry* articulated doubts about the uniqueness of the gospel. Fifteen laymen representing seven American mission boards traveled to Asia and Africa. Their report concluded that the aim of Christian missions was to "see the best in other religions, to help the adherents of those religions to discover, or to rediscover, all the best in their own traditions, to cooperate with the most active and vigorous elements in the other traditions in social reform and in the purification of religious expression. The aim should not be conversion."[1] The report was particularly detrimental to those whose understanding of the biblical basis of missions was not clear. It fostered a secular, humanistic perspective which resulted in a decline of missionary involvement in many denominations.

Describing the first half of the twentieth century, historian Stephen Neill stated, "The increasing dominance of the United States in the political affairs of the world is reflected in the vigor, generosity and vision of the American churches in the field of Christian missions."[2] The number of Protestant missionaries in the world increased four times in this period to 43,000 with two-thirds coming from the United States. Neill labeled this time the *American century for Protestant missions.*

While the missionary involvement of many historic denominations has remained somewhat constant, other boards have shown considerable increase. One agency which began at the turn of the twentieth century, for instance, has grown to include 1,300 missionaries.

During the first third of the twentieth century, the *Bible college movement* produced a large portion of missionaries and pastors for churches with non-denominational missionary support. In contrast, historic or *state churches of western Europe drastically curtailed their missions involvement.* The effect of World War I and the Hitler era all but eliminated the once strong German churches from the missionary scene. Rationalism and secularism further eroded the degree of British and Dutch involvement.

An *ecumenical emphasis* which developed in the missionary movement blurred considerably the earlier cross-cultural evangelistic concern. The theological concessions necessary for unity tended to weaken the idea of the uniqueness of the gospel in meeting man's spiritual need.

Summary

While the nineteenth century was primarily one of initiative and penetration by missions, the first half of the twentieth century was a period of consolidation. Most major areas of the world had at least been touched by the gospel. The emphasis then shifted to expanding these footholds through new churches and mission agencies working together.

The period between the world wars was also a time of recovery and preparation for new mission thrusts. Political and economic changes resulting from World War I required many adjustments, and few new mission boards were established. Instead, efforts were directed toward recovering from the trauma and upset of war. The tide of missions which had been rising before World War I was arrested for a generation and then resumed its upward direction after World War II.

Notes

1. Stephen Neill, *A History of Christian Missions,* p. 456.
2. Neill, p. 458.

For review

1. Explain the factors which contributed to making the nineteenth century "The Great Century" for missions. Are there any similar circumstances today?
2. What important contributions did Hudson Taylor and John Nevius make to missions?
3. Summarize each of the main forces and events affecting missions in the early part of the twentieth century. In what ways do these events still affect missions today?
4. Check to find out how and when the mission agency or agencies your church supports began. Discover their first fields, how they have expanded, and where their mission fields now are located.

For additional reading

Kane, J. Herbert. *A Global View of Christian Missions.* Grand Rapids: Baker Book House, 1971.
Tucker, Ruth A. *From Jerusalem to Irian Jaya.* Grand Rapids: Zondervan Publishing Company, 1983.

5

The Plan of Missions

Through the years churches have developed a variety of mission strategies. It is therefore important that we have a clear understanding of God's plan for missions as presented in the Bible and the role He has for us in the work He is accomplishing today.

Goal of missions

Missions is more than a combination of good things done by well-intentioned people for the poor and helpless. Biblical missions focuses on meeting man's spiritual need and, in the context of the church, leading him to the place where he can be used of God to meet the needs of others. Several aspects of missions often run concurrently. While evangelism is the initial concern in a new area, this should not stop when discipling begins. Discipling, in turn, continues once a church is established.

Evangelism

Presence evangelism (demonstrating Christianity through a life witness), proclamation evangelism (verbally communicating the terms of the gospel), and persuasion evangelism (actively seeking a postive response) are all phases of effective evangelism.

The one evangelizing must be aware of the progression in a person's understanding of the gospel. The process of making a decision for Christ begins with an awareness of a supreme being and culminates with the new believer evangelizing and discipling others.[1]

Discipling

While proclamation of the gospel is essential to the missionary task, it is also important to build up believers and train them to have a spiritual impact on their neighbors. The command of Christ in Matthew 28 was basically to disciple. From the book of Acts and the Epistles, we learn that the first churches obeyed this command.

We may preach the gospel, win converts, establish churches, build buildings, instruct and baptize believers; but still fail to disciple. In John 8:31, Jesus emphasized that a disciple continues in the Word. He learns to use Scripture as his resource for information and guidance and applies it in his life. A disciple also loves the brethren. Evidence of right relationships identifies disciples before the watching world. The resources and relationships available to disciples are attractive to others, resulting in a multiplication of converts.

Discipling is intended to mature converts and generate continuous evangelism. "And he gave some...pastors and teachers, for the perfecting of the saints for the work of the ministry, for the edifying of the body of Christ" (Eph. 4:11, 12, NKJV). Each member of the body of Christ possesses appropriate gifts. When the body is functioning properly, spiritual maturity and reproduction will result.

Establishing churches

The book of Acts and the Epistles indicate that the believer's membership in the church of Christ is to be reflected in his involvement with a local fellowship of believers. When he is born again, he becomes part of a church family whose members normally are nearby and of the same culture and language.

As a missionary wins people to Christ and disciples them, he leads them into the formation of a group of believers who share a common relationship with Christ. Whatever the size or structure, such a group is essential for the kind of ministry, teaching, support, and impact on the world that Christ planned for His people. It is within this local church that discipling is most productive and through its outreach that evangelism is most effective.

Result of missions

Missionaries evangelize across cultural barriers and establish churches made up of converts from the culture involved. What kind of church should be established? What should be the continuing role and relationship of the mission and missionaries to that church? Answers to these questions will largely determine how we support missions, how we pray for missions, and how and why we continue to send missionaries from our churches.

The indigenous church

Since World War II, there has been an increasing emphasis on making established churches autonomous or establishing indigenous churches which are self-governing, self-supporting, and self-propagating.[2] Building on the work of Henry Venn (1796-1893) and Rufus Anderson

(1796-1880), Roland Allen and John L. Nevius applied the concept of indigenous churches in China and Korea respectively. Although Nevius' visit to Korea in 1890 had a great impact, little attention was paid to these ideas of self-government, self-support, and self-propagation until the period between the world wars when colonialism was coming to an end. As the post-World War II political independence movement gained momentum, this concept began to dominate mission strategy. Such slogans as "train the national to take over" and "we should be working ourselves out of a job" expressed the mood of the day. Establishing indigenous churches was partly a reaction against the tendency of the colonial era to westernize, both in culture and control, the churches established by Western personnel. Allen and Nevius perceived that the life and structure of the church must fit its own cultural setting and that its leaders must be developed from within its membership.

The majority of churches around the world today are basically indigenous. Although they generally are governed and supported by local people, two concerns remain: a general failure to emphasize the recruitment and training of missionaries by national churches and the degree and type of outside financial help most beneficial to national churches.

The early church, with its initiative and innovation, provides helpful examples of church planting, especially at Corinth and the cities of Galatia. Although the New Testament records the expansion of the church across cultural barriers, these were not usually as formidable as those in most cross-cultural evangelistic situations today.[3] The Apostle Paul always emphasized the development of local leadership and responsibility, but he did not hesitate to return and intervene as needed to ensure purity and doctrine and practice. This is illustrated in his letters to the Galatians and the Corinthians.

In avoiding both paternalism (an undue continuing father role) and orphanism (a lack of any father role), Paul demonstrated the way in which God develops indigenous churches. The church at Thessalonica is an excellent example of believers who had seen the model of the missionary for just a few weeks, and then went on to imitate him in love, faith, good works, and evangelism. The quality of life and effectiveness of this church in evangelism had an impact all over Greece.

In the last quarter of the twentieth century, the establishment of indigenous churches is not as significant an issue as it was in the 1950s and 1960s. There is a new concern for the relation of mission agencies to the self-governing churches they have established. These churches in turn need to develop their own means for effective mission involvement.

With the disappearance of the colonial era and the establishment of independent national governments in almost every country of the world, it is assumed that churches established by missionaries are at least self-governing. The extent to which they are self-supporting and self-propagating varies widely from country to country and church to church. The effectiveness of indigenous churches must be measured not by the extent to which their government is autonomous but, rather, by the extent to which they are able to mobilize their personnel and involve them in effective evangelism both nearby and in other countries.

Church organization

The church which a missionary establishes in another culture usually reflects his home church. Denominational missionaries establish parallels of their denominations in overseas countries and encourage church constitutions similar to those used in their sending churches. Independent and non-denominational missionaries tend to encourage an independent, congregational form of government.

While it is understandable that each tradition considers its structure to be biblical and best, these forms do not equally fit or meet the customs and needs of people in another culture. An African group, for instance, accustomed to elders making decisions, may have trouble with total democracy.

The function of the local church in any culture needs to emphasize the basic biblical teaching that each believer is a member of the body of Christ with individual gifts and responsibilities. The form of local church government needs to relate to basic cultural patterns for its own development and its effectiveness in witness. Other matters such as architecture, forms of worship, training, payment of clergy, church membership, and discipline require application of biblical truth to the local situation.

Relationship of missions to the indigenous church

After establishing new indigenous churches, a mission organization faces the question of how its personnel and administration relate to the churches. Politics and events from the 1960s have made this an increasingly important issue. Although there are many adaptations of each, two basic approaches are possible: parallelism and fusion.

Parallelism

In this relationship, the mission sees itself as a foreign, temporary operation involved primarily in evangelism to initiate churches and other ministries. Parallelism is supportive of the church but does not involve itself in the administration or financing of local churches. Missionaries work under an administrator of the mission, usually a field director. While parallelism has many positive features, fusion is increasingly replacing it, often because of government or church pressure.

Fusion

With fusion, the mission ceases to exist as an administrative body in the overseas country except for such projects as schools for educating missionary children. All assets and properties are transferred to the national church whose leaders determine the work which a missionary is assigned and whether he will be asked to return after his furlough. Several large churches and missions in Third World countries have merged their administration and work in this way.

Both approaches have their supporters. Each has advantages and disadvantages. Considerations such as the history of the work in an area, governmental attitudes, the maturity and training of church leaders as well as interpersonal relationships between leaders and missionaries are probably more important than most of the theoretical points debated. Scripture does not conclusively establish either relationship since mission boards did not exist in the first century.

Deciding on an approach is a very practical and important issue, however, because it directly affects recruitment, financing, and, above all, the effectiveness of the spiritual thrust. In some areas where fusion has occurred, adjustments by missionaries and church leaders have been difficult, especially where mission projects were only distantly related to the life of the church. The structure of church/mission relationships is important primarily as it affects evangelizing and establishing new churches. Therefore, it is essential that all concerned continue to strive toward these goals rather than toward determining ideal structures or relationships.

Characteristics of mission strategy

Four basic dynamics which characterize all mission strategy are especially significant. They emphasize that missions is a global enterprise and recognize that man is initially more conscious of his physical than of his spiritual needs. From both a biblical and contemporary perspective, missions is:

Cross-cultural

Missions implies a communication of the gospel to those of another culture and language. Although all communication of spiritual truth may be thought of as cross-cultural, it is helpful to reserve the term *missions* primarily for evangelism in cross-cultural situations involving language barriers. This basic strategy involves contextualizing the gospel and forming churches which fit the cultural setting of converts. Contextualization is considered more fully in chapter 10.

International

Missions increasingly involves believers in many countries around the world. Although almost two-thirds of all missionaries come from North America, the number being sent by churches in Africa, Asia, and South America is steadily growing.

Cooperative

Missions requires people with a variety of skills and professions to contribute individually and collectively to the spiritual welfare of the people among whom they work. The missionary thrust is a team operation where each member makes an important contribution, whether in evangelism, education, medicine, or other activities. In work as full-time evangelists, church-planters, and Bible teachers, or as part of a support group, missionaries share in the process of bringing people to Christ and discipling them to become reproducing members of His body. For this reason, it is important that all missionaries relate themselves in an active way to the life of the local church on the field.

Coordinating the diversity of ministries available requires careful planning. Mission and church leaders must develop strategy to meet the needs and circumstances of their area. Usually medical, educational, printing, radio, and other ministries are most effective when used in a combination with each other as well as with direct evangelism and Bible teaching.

Holistic

Missions is concerned with meeting the needs of the whole man. The mission hospital/clinic and the mission school have long been identified with missionary activity. For over a century, medical work has brought healing to the body, demonstrated Christian compassion, enhanced the prestige of the church, and led to conversions. A corresponding impact has been made through educational work.

Both thrusts, however, are undergoing considerable change. National governments are taking increased responsibility for medical and educational services. Mobile clinics are growing in number. Involvement of expatriate teachers in government schools, especially at higher levels, is rising. While conditions vary greatly from country to country, the trend in missionary medical and educational work is toward mobility, short-term assignments, and specialization. National churches and governments often welcome such assistance. The extent and impact of medicine and education on the goals of evangelism, discipling, and church planting, however, depend on the goals, training, and spiritual commitment of the mission personnel involved.

In recent years, relief programs have been added to missionary concerns. Disasters, famines, and political disruptions have elicited overwhelming response from Christians in other countries. Many have contributed to rebuilding homes and churches. In addition, several organizations are helping people develop their own resources by demonstrating methods to improve farming and business techniques and by educating in ways to increase income. These funds enable the people to provide the financial resources necessary for their churches. A question arises concerning the amount of direct involvement mission agencies should commit themselves to and the extent to which they should cooperate with relief groups on the field.

Evangelical mission boards are deeply concerned with whole-man needs of the people where they work, yet want nothing to divert them from primary goals related to meeting eternal spiritual needs. In determining the direction of their church investments, pastors and church missionary committees have a heavy responsibility in weighing these two concerns from a biblical perspective.

Summary

Jesus' promise "I will build My church" (Matt. 16:18) and Paul's statement that church leaders were given "for the equipping of the saints . . . to the building up of the body of Christ" (Eph. 4:12) summarize the plan of missions for all ages. The church is both the goal and the means of evangelizing and discipling. Because He is building His church in a world of cultural compartments, each with its limitations and potentials, it is essential that the gospel be demonstrated and communicated in ways each can understand.

Because Jesus has delegated this undertaking to the church, He has equipped each member of the body, in whatever cultural surroundings, with ability to contribute. Thus, missions is the flow of the Spirit's work to fulfill Christ's promise for the glory of the Father through His people everywhere.

Notes

1. See James F. Engel and H. Wilbert Norton, *What's Gone Wrong With the Harvest?*, p. 45.
2. *Webster's New Collegiate Dictionary*, 3d ed., "indigenous: produced, growing or living naturally in a particular region or environment."
3. See Acts 18:1-18, 1 Corinthians concerning Corinth, Acts 14:21-25 concerning cities of Galatia. For cultural issues see Acts 14:6-18 and Acts 18.

For review

1. What does Jesus' command mean in Matthew 28:19? How should it be carried out in missions today?
2. What is an indigenous church? How has this idea developed over the last century?
3. What are the alternatives in the relationship between churches and missions? How do mission boards your church supports relate to churches overseas?
4. Explain four basic characteristics of mission strategy.

For additional reading

Stott, John R. W. *Christian Missions in the Modern World*. Downers Grove, IL: Intervarsity Press, 1976.

6

The Context of Missions

Missionaries must live, work, and relate to men and women in the world at their point of need. Sensitivity to these needs requires an understanding of how missions relates to our changing world. For instance, how has the great independence movement since World War II affected missions and national churches? Are there implications for missions in how other countries view North America? What effect do economic changes and the need for oil have on missions?

As we consider these and other issues, we will see that each is important. Although some may appear threatening, all "have turned out for the greater progress of the gospel" (Phil. 1:12). In the midst of pressures and perplexities, not in a hothouse or a vacuum, the power of the gospel can be recognized and the church strengthened.

Independence movement following World War II

The greatest impact on missions in recent years has resulted from over seventy-five former European colonies gaining their independence. The disillusionment of non-European peoples with the major powers involved in World War II combined with the growing freedom from overseas control created a new hope, a new spirit, and new issues and problems in large areas of the world. During the post-war years, Africa alone changed from 95 percent of its countries being under colonial rule to almost all being independent.

Political factors

Most new nations have found democracy difficult to maintain. The leader who won independence often had to face the problem of tribalism. For a president from one tribe to gain the loyalty and support of scores of tribes has often proved more difficult than gaining independence from a colonial power. Nationalism, that sense of identity and feeling of unity as a nation, has not always been easy to develop. Lack of the proper type of nationalism tends to foster fear and turmoil. Since tribalism is often blamed for this instability, the missionary who works with one tribe is sometimes caught in the middle, especially when he is translating the Bible into a local language.

Importance for missions

Newly-independent nations around the world are seeking identity, respect, and a higher standard of living for their people. Either directly or indirectly, the gospel has much to contribute toward meeting those needs. Opportunities for missionary activity have increased markedly in the past quarter of a century. Although local political and religious factors have occasionally interfered, the urgent need for technical help and the unselfish concern of missionaries have opened many doors for the gospel. Relief involvement in national disasters and droughts also has facilitated entrance of the gospel in such places as the Sudan and Bangladesh.

Independence often has brought greater respect for missionaries, especially those who remained and moved forward with national development. While the issuance of visas and work permits has been complicated by the need to protect employment opportunities for the citizens of each country, much of sub-Sahara Africa, for instance, is receptive to medical and educational work as well as church-related ministries.

Almost every country which recently has gained independence has experienced serious political unrest and often a change of government by force. In several instances, internal strife has disrupted mission work. Yet in daily local contacts, personal relationships between missionaries and nationals generally remain positive. This is especially evident where good relationships exist between the mission and church and there is mutual respect between leaders. At times, though, the political scene is carried over into church affairs. When tensions in mission/church relationships develop, they usually parallel those of the national independence movements.

Decline of North American image and influence

Justly or unjustly, the United States often has been cast as reactionary and unsympathetic to independence movements. Its image was considerably diminished in the eyes of many non-Western nations by the Vietnam conflict. Communists and other detractors attempt to picture the United States as imperialistic, neo-colonial, and not to be trusted by the common people. The affluence of North America tends to increase the suspicion of countries living at subsistence levels. The tremendous economic expansion of other industrial nations and the energy crisis, however, have proportionately diminished the power and influence of North America.

How the peoples of the world perceive the United States relates directly to the thrust of missions because a high percentage of missionaries presently come from North America. Being American is not necessarily a handicap, nor is it automatically an advantage. Those concerned with worldwide evangelization must be increasingly sensitive to the cultures and values of other peoples and be biblically based in their message and methods.

A North American needs to guard against giving the impression that his culture is superior to all others. Having conveniences and comforts does not offer the security and satisfaction which can come only from citizenship in heaven. The expatriate missionary must be sensitive to and appreciative of the values of other cultures and let Christ use His Word to make believers what He intends them to be in their cultural setting.

Commercial expansion and economic tensions

Although missionary activity in Europe has increased markedly since the war, most missionary involvement has been concentrated in developing countries, such as the new nations of Africa and Southeast Asia and the older republics of Latin America. In recent years, unprecedented developments in these areas have significantly affected the economic and social contexts. Economic changes, such as inflation, industrialization, and urbanization, affect daily life at least as much as frequent political changes.

Missionaries and national believers must adapt to these powerful forces if they are to gain a hearing for the gospel and develop strong churches. With regard to missions and growth of the church, economic and cultural concerns are more important in many countries than political considerations.

Large foreign investments by the United States, Germany, Japan, and other industrial nations in developing countries have increased the availability of consumer goods but also produced a spiraling cost of living. Limited educational facilities and local capital to invest tend to widen the gap between the "haves" and "have nots." Many are reaching levels of living higher than ever thought possible, but many more remain hopelessly destitute.

The social, spiritual, and psychological impact of commercial development is evident in much of the world; materialism, urbanization, secularism, and alienation within families have resulted. The kaleidescope of radios, tape recorders, television sets, motorcycles, cars, Western-style clothes, records, movies, books, appliances, and gadgets has revolutionized value systems and vocations in both large cities and remote villages.

Life in developing countries is not always primitive. The daily decisions and basic issues facing both missionaries and nationals often closely parallel those of North Americans. The believer whose values reflect his submission to the Lordship of Christ and who knows how to apply the Word in his own culture is the one who will be able to serve most productively.

Islam and Middle East politics

The growing demand for oil has greatly increased the visibility and resources of Islamic countries while the confrontation with Israel has tended to unify otherwise fragmented Arab nations. As a result, accelerated rates of inflation and increased involvement by Muslim leaders in the internal affairs of neighboring countries have developed. Petrodollars are financing an aggressive Islamic movement in Africa and Asia. With its polygamy and other concepts familiar to many African cultures, Islam competes for recognition as "the right religion" for the African continent.

Islamic initiatives are not limited to the non-Western world.[1] Massive investments of Arab petro-dollars in Great Britain and the United States are facilitating an effective impact for Islam. Two million Muslims now live in Britain. One militant branch has launched a missionary crusade to include "the evangelization of committed Christians."[2] Disproving the divinity of Christ is one of their basic aims.

Islam claims two million adherents in the United States, with at least fifteen mosques in New York City alone. As in Africa, they have made a concerted attempt to identify with the black community. Christianity is presented as racist and white.[3]

Islam, however, is neither monolithic nor impregnable. The distance from Mecca and Saudi Arabia seems to affect the character and intensity of Islamic values and the degree of commitment to them. Weaknesses are appearing which give increasing incentive to developing new strategies for winning Muslims to Christ. One of the most hopeful areas is southern West Africa where thousands of believers in indigenous churches are showing a real concern for winning their Islamic neighbors to Christ.

Impact of communism

Communism became an international force in World War II as Russia gained new stature among the nations for its part in defeating Germany. Then, in 1949, China fell to communist control. Communism has made considerable progress in Latin America, Cuba, many African countries, and the Far East. The involvement of both Russia and China in African affairs has resulted in unstable conditions in several countries.

Next to Islam, communism stands as the most determined and aggressive enemy of Christianity. As in the days of Roman persecution, communism must not be viewed simply as a threat to missions but rather as an expression of the satanic opposition which has always challenged the gospel. Yet, it can impede the growth of the church no more than God permits. As He has done many times in the past, God is using opposition to purify and motivate the visible church. Sustained affluence, ease, and security have seldom been the context in which strong, biblical churches have flourished and evangelized.

Communism decisively challenges Christianity at almost every point of its existence and theology. It is built on class hatred, while Christ taught radical love. Communism has no scruples against use of the most barbaric force to gain its ends while the Christian witness is limited to affectionate persuasion, with the Crusades as a notable exception.

The Bible gives the Christian his values and perspective on life while the Communist draws his life views and his strategy for conquest from the writings of Marx, Engels, Lenin, or Mao. The Christian is called upon to deny himself and devote his full efforts toward worldwide proclamation of the Christian good news. The Communist must be willing to sacrifice personal convenience for the attainment of party goals.

Today vast stretches of the earth's surface and masses of population are under the control of communist governments. Approximately one-third of the world's peoples are living under communist regimes.[4] These masses include the most populous nation, China, and the world's largest country, the Union of Soviet Socialist Republics, whose land mass spans eleven time zones.

Churches in communist countries vary in relation to their respective governments. Considerable religious freedom is experienced in Poland, Nicaragua, and Yugoslavia whereas limited freedom to worship, job discrimination, and educational difficulties are the lot of Christians in East Germany and Cuba. Governmental registration of churches with a parallel development of unregistered "underground" churches is the hallmark in the USSR, China, Romania, and Bulgaria. In Ethiopia and Vietnam the churches face severe persecution, while in Laos, Cambodia, Mongolia, and Albania visible religious activity has been virtually eliminated.[5] Yet almost everywhere among communist nations the church continues to grow, attracting the old, the young, and even Communist party members.

The doors of witness to communist nations may be closed at the border crossing to the traditional missionary, but they are open to broadcasting, postal mailers, and creative Christian witnesses who dare to climb over man-made barriers to fulfill the Great Commission.

Christians within communist lands commonly experience persecution. Incarceration in mental hospitals, removal of children from homes of Christian parents, arrest, prosecution, and imprisonment of evangelical leaders, and occasionally death by torture are current persecution techniques. These repressive measures seem only to illustrate the truth of the Soviet proverb, "Religion is like a stake in the ground. The harder you strike it, the deeper it goes."

Christians everywhere are responsible to intercede before God for believers in communist nations, requesting that they be protected, encouraged, and energized in their Christian faithfulness and witness. Many Christians are seeking to involve themselves in efforts to exert moral pressure on communist governments by means of appeals to governmental authorities and use of the mass media to publicize specific instances of harrassment and intolerance. A forgetful or unconcerned spirit reveals either an unnecessary ignorance or an unbelieving acceptance of their plight.

Summary

When Jesus interceded for His disciples the night before the crucifixion, He said to the Father, "My prayer is not that you take them out of the world but that you protect them from the evil one . . . . As you have sent me into the world, I have sent them into the world" (John 17:15, 18, NIV).

The world into which Jesus sent His men was a hostile, hurting civilization plagued with political unrest and economic uncertainty. Many of the issues and concerns of that day are still with us. The difference lies in today's rate of change and intensification of the troubles and traumas which multiply with the world's population.

Undoubtedly the early church survived and grew because it understood the concerns of the day. Empowered by the Holy Spirit, it reached out to men in need. If we are to do the same, we must understand the times in which we live, especially the context and conditions in which worldwide evangelization is taking place. It will then be the same Holy Spirit who shows us how to respond to new conditions, to innovate, and to overcome Satan's obstacles.

Notes

1. *Muslim World Pulse,* vol. VII, no. 2, April 1978.
2. *Christianity Today,* January 13, 1978, p. 57.
3. *Muslim World Pulse,* vol. VII, no. 2, April 1978, pp. 3, 4.
4. Patrick Johnstone, *Operation World,* p. 70
5. Johnstone, p. 71.

For review

1. What is nationalism? How does it relate to the development of missions following World War II?
2. In what specific ways do commercial expansion and economic tensions affect missions?
3. How should the church prepare for communist pressure and attack?

For additional reading

Barrett, David R̈., ed. *World Christian Encyclopedia.* New York: Oxford University Press, 1982.

Frizen, Edwin L. and Coggins, Wade T. *Christ and Caesar in Christian Missions.* Pasadena, CA: William Carey Library, 1979.

7

The Sending Church

Missions involves worldwide expansion of the church. The human initiative and responsibility needed in supplying personnel and funds for
the spread of the gospel rests primarily with the local church. Although
resources and opportunities vary, all churches have the potential to
become sending churches.

In the first century, believers from Jerusalem brought the gospel to
Antioch; that church in turn sent Barnabas and Saul to Asia Minor and
Europe. In the twentieth century, the pattern continues. Third World
churches established by missionaries from Western countries are sending people across cultural and geographical barriers and giving them
support to reach other groups. Yet, applying Christ's teaching in Luke
12:48 that "to whom they entrusted much, of him they will ask all the
more" lays a heavy responsibility on churches in countries where
resources for training and supporting personnel are abundant.

Not only does the missions thrust depend on the local church, but the
church must be involved in missions to fulfill its own purpose. Serious,
growing mission involvement is both a cause and effect of vibrant
spiritual life in a congregation.

Responsibilities of leaders

Mission success is closely related to activity in the sending church.
The degree and quality of activity is largely influenced by its leadership.

Establish policy

While some churches feel that a written missions policy is restrictive
or unnecessary and others have given it little or no thought, the Holy
Spirit can and does guide in both the formation and implementation of
appropriate guidelines. Thinking through a missions policy testifies to
the church's serious commitment to fulfill its responsibility in worldwide evangelization.[1]

A stated policy tends to build confidence and encourage coordination
of effort. It defines reponsibilities and makes possible the planning nec-

essary for development of an effective missions program. It also allows for thoughtful evaluation of crucial issues and tends to eliminate emotional, pressured, or inconsistent decisions.

Set example

Although the pastor should not be the only voice for missions in the church, his concern should be evident in practical, effective ways. By modeling a personal missionary concern and monitoring the whole missions program of his church, he is in a position to give strong leadership in encouraging congregational interest and involvement.

Plan

Some churches look to the elders or deacons for guidance in their missions emphasis. Many churches, however, realize the benefits of establishing a missions committee to give concentrated attention to this important priority. The purpose of the missions committee is not to relieve the pastor, the official boards, or the congregation of their missionary responsibility, but rather to plan total church involvement and give the attention needed for the various missions functions to be effective.

The selection of committee members, their qualifications, terms of service, and responsibilities should be considered in light of the needs and resources of the congregation. A balance between the continuity gained from long terms of service on the committee and the involvement of many people might be achieved by rotation of membership. In addition to a keen missions interest, all members need to be aware of the foundations of missions and current developments.

A cabinet structure offers many benefits to a missions committee. In this arrangement, each committee member is given responsibility for one basic function. He may involve others in the undertaking while he coordinates activities with other committee members.

Responsibilities of the church

Most Christians have only vague ideas concerning the goals of missions. Their understanding of what is involved in communicating the gospel and establishing churches cross-culturally is limited. Local churches are responsible both for informing their people regarding missions and developing missionary interest.

Educate in missions

If congregations are to increase participation in missions, they need continuing, accurate, and effective teaching about missions. This is especially true today when the world scene and mission strategy are changing so rapidly. The more people know about what needs to be done and how it can be accomplished, the more they are likely to involve themselves in praying, giving, and making themselves available for service.

Many practical means are available for a continual program of educating the church in missions.

- The pastor can set the pace for teaching missions by occasionally giving a series of *messages* on the biblical basis of missions and making frequent references to current mission developments. When speaking on other themes and scriptural passages, he can show their implications for missions.

- Most *Sunday school curricula* include courses in missions. When the material is current and the teacher well informed, this is an effective way of teaching missions to various age groups. When mission executives or teachers of missions are available in the area, church leaders should plan special sessions for them to inform and interact with Sunday school teachers concerning missions.

- *Reports* by visiting missionaries are personal and specific. In addition, letters and cassettes can provide current information during a church service. Preparing special news reports from this information also provides opportunity to involve various members of the congregation.

- A *church library* should be well stocked with basic and current literature on missions. Biographies are good but should not dominate the holdings.

- At least one large, carefully maintained *world map* showing the location of missionaries whom the church supports should be prominently displayed. It also can provide statistical information and point out unreached peoples needing prayer. Large-scale maps showing areas where each supported missionary serves also may be featured. These maps make geographical references in prayer letters more understandable.

- Many churches schedule one *mission conference* each year and supplement it with several other weekends of mission emphasis. The goals and format of a conference should vary from year to year to meet congregational needs.

- To learn of missions, people need a *file of current information* on such subjects as the personnel and financial needs of mission boards, missionary training institutions, and opportunities in missions. These files should be easy to use and accessible to church youth. Church leaders can encourage use of the files by personal example and public reference to them.

- Pastors and members of a congregation, especially youth, *travel to mission fields* with increasing frequency. Whether for observation or short-term service, these trips should be planned carefully and used as effectively as possible to inform and inspire the whole congregation.

Identify and prepare new missionaries

The function of the missionary agency in recruiting, screening, and moving the missionary appointee to the field is well known. In the same way, most congregations are aware of the work of the training institution in teaching the prospective missionary biblical studies, Christian living principles, the basics of missions, and other appropriate subjects. Often, however, the church fails to realize that members of its congregation are in a position to make a unique contribution in selecting and preparing new missionaries for the field. Specific ways to do this follow.

Give a young person information concerning mission opportunities and share how his involvement could be helpful. Vocational guidance for teens and young adults is often an overlooked responsibility and privilege of church leaders. Such assistance can help establish and apply a biblical value system based on the priority of God's leading in his life, an emphasis not likely to be included in a secular educational program. Counseling of this nature can discourage inappropriate volunteering, especially that done as an emotional response by unqualified persons.

Challenge persons who evidence spiritual gifts, maturity, and effective experience in ministry since these are possible indications of the Lord's intention for them to enter vocational Christian service. The Apostle Paul demonstrated this when he recruited Timothy in Lystra on the recommendation of the church leaders who knew him well. In addition, many qualified persons conscious of their limitations need older, respected friends in the church to express the confidence and conviction that God can use them in missions. Michael Griffiths makes this point well:

> But others need objective confirmation of their own genuine subjective sense of call . . . objective recognition of that call, *first,* by the congregation, or by the group of Christians who know that individual best: They know his gifts and usefulness. It may also be confirmed, *second,* by the invitation of those involved already in some distant work of evangelism and church planting.[2]

Disciple

Since Christ's command was "make disciples of all nations," those following the command must be disciples themselves. His disciples must be skilled at making more disciples. It is helpful if the discipling process already has been experienced personally. No matter how well educated or qualified he is, a missionary is not likely to produce what he is not himself, perform what he has not seen done in his home church, or accomplish what he has not been privileged to do in his own culture.

Discipling involves teaching, training, and, above all, demonstrating through a disciplined life the truths being taught. In the New Testament, the local church was primarily responsible for developing the individual.

The believers at Thessalonica, for instance, were taught in the Word and doctrine and followed Paul's example. His discipling helped them become disciplers of people throughout Greece.

Pray

Since the first missionary church in Antioch, prayer has been the dynamic of missions. In response to the prayer of believers, God often has intervened in the warfare against Satan so that missions can have penetrating power. Therefore, believers need to intercede for many aspects of missionary activity.

When Jesus saw the needy multitudes, in compassion He commanded, "Beseech the Lord of the harvest *to send out workers* into His harvest." If all churches obeyed this command, a totally adequate missionary force could be continuously supplied without human pressure. This procedure for missionary recruitment would include the whole church and create widespread joy in participation as well as give recognition to the Lord who makes the appointment to service.

Michael Griffiths points out:

> But if a church, a congregation, has together prayed and sought the will of God to know which of their gifted young couples, which leader of their youth work or men's group, they should send, then two people intimately known to them . . . have gone out. They (the congregation) will pray not for initials but for friends who are facing difficulties now because they sent them where they are and are thus very responsible to pray for them.[3]

Thanksgiving for the opportunity to be involved in missions and intercession for specific issues, decisions, and *needs of church-supported missionaries* are important parts of prayer. Missionaries also need prayer for spiritual, psychological, and physical strength, for their interpersonal relationships, and, above all, for boldness in witness.

National church leaders need much prayer. This is especially true of those known to the sending church, such as businessmen, teachers, and others in overseas congregations. Often they have the same concerns and needs as those who pray for them at home.

The unevangelized need concentrated prayer. Four-fifths of all the unreached in the world today do not live in a place where the gospel is readily available to them. There also are areas which have a gospel witness, but those around have not yet heard it.

A church which prays effectively for missions does not limit its intercession to church services. To facilitate family prayer, a missionary prayer board mounted where the family eats and/or prays helps greatly. Pictures of missionaries, maps, urgent prayer requests, and progress charts of family missionary giving can be included on the board.

Support financially

When a church is fulfilling its other mission responsibilites, financial support is not a burden. In Matthew 6:20, 21 Jesus emphasized the importance of giving our money for eternal values when He said, "Lay up for yourselves treasures in heaven . . . for where your treasure is, there will your heart be also." People with a heart for missions will invest joyfully.

Policy decisions are needed in two main aspects of mission financing—how funds are generated and on what basis they are dispersed. Most churches plan their missionary budget from one of five basic sources:

- a percentage of the church's total giving
- the previous year's missions giving, usually with an increase included for added costs
- pledges made at an annual conference
- an annual offering for missions
- a faith/promise commitment in which an unsigned promise is made to give what the individual trusts God to provide through him during the coming year

Each system has advantages and disadvantages. Total church giving devoted to missions tends to increase as people learn of mission needs, have personal contact with mission personnel, and act on faith that God wants to work through them. This is especially true when the congregation is spiritually alive, has a biblically-based concern for the spiritual condition of the lost, and understands its responsibility in reaching them.

Denominational leaders use three basic patterns of missions support.

- All money is given to the denomination's mission account. A church may have special interest in a specific missionary and consider it is supporting him through the fund, but the local church does not determine who or what the fund supports.
- Contributions are made to the denominational missions program, but also to the support of persons and projects under non-denominational faith boards.
- All funds go to personalized support, such as the financial needs of an individual or family chosen by the church.

Churches in the latter two categories usually establish criteria for determining which missionaries and projects to support. Many considerations are involved and policies differ from church to church.

Care for missionaries on furlough

Furlough is not a vacation for missionaries, although substantial time should be reserved for rest and relaxation. This is a time for renewal of family, church, and personal relationships; sharing what God has been doing on the field; gaining perspective on the work; updating knowledge and skills; and refreshing the spirit for future service.[4]

The practical hospitality and assistance provided by supporting churches can greatly influence the benefits of the furlough period and the spirit with which the missionary returns to the field. A church can assist in a variety of ways.

• Guide the missionary and his family in adjustments to new and unfamiliar developments that have occurred during his absence.
• Arrange housing and transportation as required.
• Provide pastoral care through counseling, encouraging, and fellowshipping with the missionary and members of his family.
• Have the pastor's wife give special help as a friend and confidante to the wife or a single woman missionary.
• Encourage, arrange, and help finance continuing education.
• Prepare for return to the field by providing as much as possible for financial and other needs.

Summary

The mission-oriented church will demonstrate its commitment to those priorities and programs basic to worldwide evangelization by fulfilling the responsibilities for leaders and churches listed in the chapter. Much time and effort must be exerted to inform the congregation of the value of missions, to identify and prepare new missionaries, to disciple fellow believers, to bathe each activity in prayer, to provide financial support for those in need, and to care for furloughing missionaries. As care and concern are demonstrated for those in our circle of influence, an increasing sensitivity can be developed for brothers and sisters around the world.

Resources

How to Organize a Mission Program in the Local Church, Louis Neibauer Company, Inc., Jenkintown, PA 19046.

Association of Church Missions Committees, P.O. Box ACMC, Wheaton, IL 60189-8000.

Evangelical Missions Information Service, P.O. Box 794, Wheaton, IL 60189.

Missions Advanced Research & Communication Center, 919 West Huntington Drive, Monrovia, CA 91016.

Notes

1. For helpful procedures and guidelines in developing missions policy, see *Missions Policy Handbook*, available from the Association of Church Missions Committees.
2. Michael Griffiths, *Give Up Your Small Ambitions*, pp, 20, 21.
3. Griffiths, p. 22.
4. See Marjorie A. Collins, *Who Cares About the Missionary?*, pp. 61-91.

For review

1. With what mission responsibilities should a local church concern itself?
2. How may mission education be carried out in a local church? How could you implement these in your church?
3. What is the responsibility of the local church in recruiting and preparing missionaries?
4. How may a church finance missions? Which method does your church use? Discuss its effectiveness.
5. What are practical ways that your church can assist your missionaries when they are on furlough?

For additional reading

Beals, Paul A. *A People for His Name: A Church/Based Missions Strategy.* Pasadena, CA: William Carey Library, 1985.

Bryant, David. *With Concerts of Prayer.* Ventura, CA: Regal Books, 1985.

Collins, Marjorie A. *Manual for Missionaries on Furlough.* Pasadena, CA: William Carey Library, 1978.

Griffiths, Michael. *God's Forgetful Pilgrims.* Grand Rapids: Eerdmans, 1975.

Wagner, C. Peter. *On the Crest of the Wave.* Glendale: Regal Books, 1983.

8

The Missionary

Without missionaries, there would be no missions. God's plan is to communicate with people through people. But what people? Is everyone a missionary? If only some are missionaries, am I to be one? What qualifications and preparation would I need? These are important questions for each believer.

Definition

While each believer has the responsibility and privilege to bear witness to Jesus Christ, we confuse our thinking if we use the word *missionary* for all Christians. Although the word is not found in Scripture, the idea of selecting and commissioning individuals for special responsibility is well illustrated in Luke 6:13, "And when day came, He called His disciples to Him; and chose twelve of them, whom He also named as apostles." The word *apostle* comes from a Greek word meaning "a sent one." While missionaries are not apostles in the New Testament sense of that word, the action of "sending with a message" is emphasized in both terms. The word *missionary* comes from the Latin parallel of apostle.

The church at Antioch illustrates a further development in the concept of a missionary. Guided by the Holy Spirit's selection, believers laid their hands on Barnabas and Saul and sent them away. They were commissioned to preach the gospel in a cross-cultural, geographically distant situation. Barnabas and Saul were *missionaries* as distinguished from *believers* who stayed in Antioch and prayed for them.

The term *missionary* is best used to refer specifically to those living and evangelizing in a distant location, usually a different culture, who are financially supported by others in their own culture. The biblical pattern also reveals that believers who are part of the process of identifying, confirming, preparing, and supporting missionaries are essential persons in missions.

Identification

How do I know if God wants me to be a missionary? Do I need a call? These and dozens of other questions could be asked by one seeking the unfolding of God's plan for his life. Specific direction will be part of

God's clear, continual leading of a submissive believer who is committed by faith to serve Him anywhere, any way, any time.

While some wait passively for a voice or a vision, others are tempted to move ahead with no divine leading. We must remember Paul's Macedonian call was not a call to be a missionary but a directive that as a veteran missionary he advance to a different field.

All believers are given responsibility as integral, gifted parts of the body of Christ. Jesus' invitation to Peter and his comrades in Luke 5:10, 11 was, in effect, an early stage of His calling these men into a full-time ministry. The Spirit gives some believers responsibilities that require all of their time while other believers are committed to provide for their physical needs.

Missionaries are believers whom God has led to serve Him full-time in another culture. Although the believer may not need a special call for this, he does require a clear leading from the Lord and confirmation of this leading from other believers.

Missionary service does not always involve locating in one place for a lifetime. In recent years, a new mobility for the missionary has become increasingly important both in short terms of service and in career appointments. The development of strong national churches, population shifts, and changing opportunities and conditions together with ease in travel have made increased flexibility both necessary and advantageous. In addition, greater numbers of people are accepting appointments for two years or less.

Conditions for guidance

God points out the path to those who have committed themselves ahead of time to walking in it. The process never ends, since God makes known plans one step at a time. Even the crucial stage of confirming the missionary role may not come suddenly but in a series of events. The selection of a mission board, decision on the nature and place of service, provision of support, and many other matters require continual dependence upon the guidance of the Holy Spirit. And this is only the beginning. Each day of ministry in a different culture, with its new situations for which there are no old solutions, makes one increasingly dependent upon the Holy Spirit's control.

To receive such guidance, continual openness and submission to the revealed will of God are needed. Concerted prayer, continual meditation in the Word, and a compliance with the indications God gives of His leading will help develop these traits.

Counsel on guidance

If one is serious about being available to God, he can express openness in several important ways. These positive steps assist in perceiving God's leading, whether or not it is toward overseas involvement

in missions.
- *Maintain mobility.* Debts and other long-term obligations, including social relationships which would preclude a move overseas, should be avoided.
- *Keep an open mind on geographical areas and types of service.* Setting boundaries in one's thinking limits God in His leading.
- *Prepare for God's leading.* To receive a call, one needs to stay within calling distance. Commitment is expected and must be continually refreshed.
- *Examine motives.* Are approval and applause from men being sought? Or is a burden from the Lord for others being accepted?
- *Make every effort to prepare for wherever God may lead.* A close walk with Him and other believers each day is essential. Seeking ways to contribute to the lives of both believers and unbelievers and to get all the education and experience possible will be beneficial.

Confirmation of guidance

While he does not need to wait for an unusual call, the Christian should be careful not to appoint himself a missionary. Pastors, teachers, and spiritually mature peers aid in assessing spiritual gifts and potentials. The response of a mission board to an application also helps determine a person's place in missions.

Qualifications

Because of the varied responsibilities of mission work, a missionary should evidence Christian characteristics in all areas of his life.

Spiritual

While a missionary is not a flawless saint, he does need to be a person of evident and unquestioned spiritual maturity. He needs to know God and how to use God's Word to meet his own needs. He needs the assurance of having applied truth in his own experience so he can take the initiative in spiritual things and have an impact on others. If he is to make a significant spiritual contribution in another culture, the power and fruit of the Spirit should be evident in his own life.

Social

Right attitudes and good interpersonal relationships are important for the missionary. He must have the kind of self-acceptance and realization of God's love that will give him confidence in relating to peers, those in authority over him, and the people among whom he ministers. There is no place for egotism, divisiveness, bitterness, complaining, prejudice, or a superior attitude.

Academic

Professional training and proficiency in medicine, education, and other support ministries are the same as those required for practice in North America. In addition, most boards require at least one year of formal Bible training for those who have not attended a Bible college or seminary. Teaching in an overseas pastoral training institution usually requires a graduate degree. For those working with churches, the more Bible education obtained, the better. Career missionaries, in most situations, must learn a new language. In all these areas, the prospective missionary should gain as much practical experience as possible after formal training.

Meeting a mission board's academic standards for acceptance does not end the need for training. On the field and on furlough, he should be involved in continuing education. Both formal and informal training increase his effectiveness, give him flexibility to meet changing situations, and prepare him for further opportunities. Training also readies him to return to his home country if the demands of family or circumstances indicate that he should leave the field for a time.

Physical and psychological

Different, demanding circumstances created by living in another country require a high level of physical stamina. Equally important are those personal qualities essential for triumph in trying circumstances. Deprived of many cultural and social anchors, the missionary needs to possess a deep emotional stability. As Kane points out, this includes adaptability, a sense of humor, a cooperative spirit, and the ability to endure hard situations while persevering with patience.[1]

An assurance of the missionary's role, a knowledge of his responsibility, and an awareness of resources together with a confidence in the One who sent him are essential ingredients for fruitful missionary service.

Preparation

How is willingness to serve transformed into actually working overseas? When a candidate becomes an appointee with a mission board, he enters some of the most exciting, demanding months of his missionary career. He has the Lord's authority to move ahead and is aware of what he needs to get to the field. He probably knows the place and work to which he is headed, but he is on a countdown which involves many unprecedented experiences and will culminate in several years of separation from his family, friends, and everything familiar. Several steps are involved in this transition.

Orientation

Most mission boards schedule an orientation period of at least two weeks for missionary candidates and appointees. Administrative and furloughing personnel provide information and interact concerning policies, procedures, and current field conditions. This orientation program serves as an excellent opportunity for evaluating the candidate as well as increasing the understanding and relationship between him and others on the team. By this time, the individual usually has made formal application to the mission board and is interviewed by appropriate staff members.

Later, when the missionary arrives on the field, he becomes involved in more specific orientation including an overview of the work in his area and introductions to colleagues, church leaders, and others in the community. These initial contacts and impressions are important. Also, intensive language study usually occupies at least a year of the first term and provides an excellent opportunity to understand and appreciate the new culture and people in the area.

Information

The appointee will find great profit in learning all he can about the people and place to which he is going and the mission personnel with whom he will be serving. It is advantageous to research the history, politics, economics, and culture of his target area as well as learn all he can about the development of the church and the progress of evangelism in the country. Although he will gain information about the mission board itself in the orientation program, getting to know future colleagues and their families by corresponding with them before arriving can build bridges for a smooth transition into the work.

Deputation

The missionary appointee usually depends upon his home church, his denomination, other groups, and individuals to provide the prayer and financial support needed. Perhaps his most important activity in the period between his appointment and his departure to the field is the deepening and strengthening of relationships with his support base. Churches and individuals need to perceive God's hand upon the appointee and make serious financial and prayer commitments on his behalf. The appointee needs to communicate his vision and commitment to potential supporters, allowing God to use him in the churches where he shares his burden. Churches need to be sensitive to opportunities the Lord gives to invest money and prayer in the life and ministry of a prospective missionary.

Relationships

A missionary's relationship to churches, to other missionaries, and within his family are vital to his personal development and to the effectiveness of his ministry.

To churches

Missions focuses on the expansion of the church worldwide. In daily relationships, though, the missionary is normally concerned with two churches—the one that sends him and the one where he ministers.

A missionary's home church should have an important part in getting him to the field and in maintaining him there.[2] This church or some other will probably commission and/or ordain him. To such groups of believers, the missionary writes reports and returns for furlough.

While the missionary needs to maintain close personal ties with a sending church, he also needs to relate to the local national church. Even in a pioneer evangelism situation, a church usually is established. It is important that the missionary identify closely with those believers whom he has gone to serve.

When a mission and church have merged on a field, the missionary works under the direction of the church. Even when merger has not taken place, he should respect and cooperate with the believers there, relating to them as the closest visible part of Christ's church. To evidence a higher loyalty to a distant church in the homeland unknown to nationals limits the effectiveness of the missionary's work, makes him appear self-directed, and demeans the spiritual gifts and potential of the people around him. On the positive side, the more closely he shares in the life of the local national church, the more he fulfills the purpose for which his home church sent him.

To other missionaries

At home one can usually choose friends and associates in Christian work or at least find a variety of compatible Christians who share a common culture and mother tongue. While serving in another culture, however, a missionary usually has a limited circle of individuals from his own culture. His social and working contacts are narrow, especially in the years before he learns the language and becomes deeply involved with the people of the area.

Christ's commission was to make disciples of all the nations. Only those who are disciples can make disciples. They are identified by their love for one another. It is therefore of greatest importance that missionaries evidence the love of Christ toward each other in all of their relationships and service. They must model the kind of life within the church that Christ intended in order to effectively plant and nourish new churches. The basis of this kind of fellowship is a consistently close walk with the Lord and a deep respect for other believers.

Within the family

In the stimulating and unpredictable experience of living together in another culture, family relationships can thrive or disintegrate. How well the parents, the father in particular, respond with constant trust and dependence on the Lord usually makes the difference. The spiritual pace and priorities he sets will influence relationships within the family and the relationship of the family to the community. Although not all family members can participate to the same extent in planning, it is important that each understands the work and feels a part of the family's ministry on the field. A sense of achievement and involvement often helps overcome tensions and temptations.

Work assigned by the mission or national church usually clearly defines the father's missionary role. The wife's role is often not so clearly laid out. Her involvement may change considerably from one term of service to another depending on her skills, the number and ages of children, and other factors which influence the extent to which she can give time to the work. In most cases, the wife can have a considerable spiritual impact in and through her home in addition to whatever other responsibilities she carries.

The parents' attitudes toward such matters as their work, local people, and other missionaries make a great impression on their children. A child growing up in two cultures has a special need for security. He can only receive that assurance from secure parents whose relationships and values reflect a sense of being sent by God.

Education can be a problem for a missionary child (MK). In many instances, MKs can be educated on the field, especially in the urban areas of Europe or Latin America. When conditions make a boarding school education appropriate, the parents' positive attitudes are central in making it a beneficial experience for all members of the family. Decisions also must be made with regard to schooling when the family goes on furlough and when the MK is seeking higher education.

It is imperative that a husband and wife think through and understand their roles and relationships as they interact with the family unit concerning their missionary service. Adaptability and flexibility rather than stereotyped or extreme concepts should characterize their approach. A continuing appreciation for the privilege of serving together in a work with eternal value helps put problems in perspective and provides the incentive for overcoming hazards.

Summary

People are the basic instrument in cross-cultural communication of the gospel. Yet, missions requires supernatural motivation, guidance, gifts, abilities, and resources. The whole process by which believers are led into missionary service and supported through prayer and finances is a faith experience. For the sending church and the missionary, it represents a high privilege and a significant investment.

Considering the eternal significance of missions, it is amazing that God uses people—people with weaknesses and limitations. Yet, God leads and empowers as they carry a message of eternal importance to an unfamiliar culture. When difficult circumstances arise, the missionary needs to be certain of God's leading, aware of his own responsibilities, prepared for his work, and rightly related to the people around him. Above all, he needs to live the message he preaches. In 1 Thessalonians 1:5, the Apostle Paul expressed his standard, "For our gospel did not come to you in word only, but also in power and in the Holy Spirit and with full conviction; just as you know what kind of men we proved to be among you for your sake."

Notes

1. Herbert Kane, *Understanding Christian Missions*, pp. 77, 78.
2. Edwin Frizen, "Missionaries and Their Sending Churches", *Evangelical Missions Quarterly*, Vol. 16, No. 2, April, 1980, p. 69.

For review

1. Define *missionary* with reference to Luke 6:13 and Acts 13:3.
2. How would you respond to the statement: "I do not have a missionary call so God doesn't want me to be a missionary"?
3. What steps are involved in getting a missionary to his field of service? How can a missionary's home church and mission board cooperate to help him in this process?
4. What steps can a family take to make service in another culture a positive experience?

For additional reading

Kane, J. Herbert. *Life and Work on the Mission Field.* Grand Rapids; Baker Book House, 1980.

9

Recent Developments in Mission Strategy

The increased importance of national churches following World War II and the opportunity for the advance of missions as the world's population exploded created a crisis in mission methodology. Workable, biblical answers could herald a new age for church growth, but maintaining the status quo would result in stagnation or reduced effectiveness. What was to be done?

Unprecedented breakthroughs in the expansion of the church and training of leaders began in the early 1960s. The impact of the application of these biblical principles continues to increase and influence missionary strategy today. Three separate movements share common emphases in their involvement of believers, decentralized activity apart from church buildings, and concern for the growth and development of the church as the functioning body of Christ.

While the message of the gospel is "absolute, perfect and final . . . . the practices of proclamation are man-related and therefore are relative. They are conditioned by the messenger and the psychology and sociology of the people to whom the gospel is being proclaimed."[1] *Saturation evangelism* emphasizes the motivation, mobilization, and involvement of multitudes of believers in effectively making Christ known. The *church growth movement* is greatly concerned with the expansion of the church in terms of new converts and new congregations. Finally, *TEE* (theological education by extension) provides training in the Word and church-related skills to a much broader group of believers than the few resident students who can be educated in institutions.

Saturation evangelism

Because of its outstanding results, application to varying cultures, and church-centered foundation, saturation evangelism is an important development in this century. The idea of involving the whole church in evangelism has many historic precedents. The early church grew because a high proportion of its members evangelized aggressively. Soon after Pentecost they had filled Jerusalem with their teaching. All who lived in Asia heard the Word. Later tens of thousands turned to the Lord. Luke verifies that this phenomenal spread of the gospel was related to the mobilization of many believers: "They that were scattered abroad went every where preaching the word" (Acts 8:4, KJV). These were not the church leaders. The chapter records that "they were all scattered abroad throughout the regions of Judea and Samaria, except the apostles."

Saturation evangelism is a part of the history of the church. In 1527, for instance, the Anabaptists led the way not only in sending teams of evangelists throughout Europe, but also in seeking to involve church members in evangelism.[2] In recent years, such movements as Evangelism In Depth in Latin America, New Life For All in Africa, and Mobilization Evangelism in Japan also have worked to accomplish the same purposes.

Today, many Christians reduce the concept of evangelism to a highly specialized activity for professionals especially gifted and trained for this work. Evangelism is thus associated primarily with mass meetings and media presentations. Saturation evangelism respects and appreciates this thrust but goes on to emphasize evangelism of even greater numbers of people by a larger number of ordinary believers. It is more person- and church-oriented than crusades or mass evangelism.

Saturation evangelism is distinct, and to some extent different, from traditional evangelism in several ways.

- It aims at saturating every area and strata of society.
- It reaches out to where the lost live.
- It involves as many evangelical groups as possible.
- It follows a coordinated schedule of simultaneous activities.

The churches involved study the spiritual understanding and needs of people in the area, mobilize their members, and develop a strategy to communicate the gospel to individuals of every age and affinity group. Every possible approach is used, including door-to-door visitation, multimedia, open-air meetings, and personal contact. The thrust is serious, aggressive, and total.

Traditional evangelism is often limited in time, place, and personnel. Church members plan a certain time to bring unsaved to the church that they may be evangelized. Saturation evangelism, on the other hand, "mobilizes and trains every believer to become an active and effective evangelizer for Christ, to go and tell the people the gospel where they are."[3]

Cooperation and mutual support encourage a sense of confidence and replace competition with concentration of effort. This climax of working together in planning, instruction, prayer, and other functions strengthens the whole undertaking and communicates to the unsaved the image of a concerned, interrelated group of witnesses.

From the first organizational and planning meetings through the instruction, mobilization, and preparation stages, the undertaking is coordinated in the cooperating churches for maximum unity of spirit and strength of impact. The evangelism stage is carefully planned and developed over a period of months with a variety of approaches to different target groups.[4]

The saturation evangelism concept has been applied in many parts of the world, but two models stand out for their pioneering strategy and their powerful impact. Evangelism In Depth, the Latin American model, originated in 1960 with Dr. Kenneth Strachan of the Latin America Mission. The eight countries first involved saw over 100,000 people come to Christ in nine years. In Africa, the New Life For All program was initiated by Gerald Swank in 1963. He and other church leaders in Nigeria studied the Evangelism in Depth approach and made appropriate adaptations for Africa. The African model was constructed on a one-year cycle of activities which was repeated for several years. This involved the sequence of preparation, information, instruction, evangelism, confirmation, and evaluation. Hundreds of interdenominational lay gospel teams penetrated unreached areas of Nigeria. In one instance, 200 volunteers led 2,000 people to salvation in Christ during one month. Many thousands came to the Lord in Nigeria despite the Biafran War. New Life For All also spread to a number of other countries in Africa.

Church growth movement

The church growth movement was sparked and popularized by Dr. Donald McGavran, a missionary to India. In 1963 he established the Institute of Church Growth at Eugene, Oregon. A few years later, it became the School of World Missions and Church Growth at Fuller Theological Seminary in California. Now that the movement is worldwide in impact, many other institutions are providing instruction in church growth principles. Most mission groups and large churches are implementing these principles in their strategy.

The concern of church growth leaders is for the increasing multiplication of converts and congregations. Basically this is an emphasis on evangelism which measurably increases church membership. It is assumed that significant growth does not just happen, but that church leaders in every culture must pray, plan, and prepare for it.

Because the movement began in the context of field activity and statistical analysis rather than in theology or Bible study, it has generated considerable investigation as well as interest.[5] In recent years, leaders of the movement have clarified some of the terminology, such as changing "people movements" to "multi-individual conversions" and have sought to provide biblical and doctrinal foundations for their principles. Whatever questions may be raised, it is clear that the undivided concern of the church growth movement remains the salvation of the lost and the building of converts into evangelizing church members.

The movement emphasizes five basic ideas:
• Increase in the number of believers as church members and develop-

ment of their spiritual growth are the church's highest priorities.
* The greatest investment of personnel and funds in evangelism should be made where people are known to be most receptive.
* The conversion of whole groups of people is possible and desirable as an evangelism strategy.
* The insights of anthropology and sociology should be applied to mission strategy, especially with regard to the communication of the gospel and the decision-making process.
* Significant growth in converts and in congregations is to be expected, projected, and planned.[6]

Many missions and church groups around the world have made use of these principles with impressive results. An effective impact has come through church growth workshops led by Dr. Vergil Gerber. By 1980 Gerber, accompanied by various team members, had led workshops in more than seventy countries. The four-day workshops are planned for representatives of national churches. Sessions emphasize biblical teaching on the role of church members, diagnosis of factors involved in growth problems by the pastors themselves, and guidance in projecting and planning for future development. Marked increases in conversions, new congregations, and church membership have resulted.[7]

Theological Education by Extension (TEE)

In 1960 the Presbyterian church of Guatamala faced a dual problem: a shortage of church leadership and a tendency for trained pastors to come to or remain in the large urban areas. As they began to evaluate training methods, seminary leaders noted that the curriculum duplicated that used in North American and European institutions. Almost all students were single male volunteers who had left their home environment to study at a centrally located institution for three years. This was the way almost all churches and missions throughout the world were training their pastors at the time.

Responding creatively to this crisis, the staff introduced a basic biblical concept which has made a worldwide impact. TEE emphasizes training church leaders, usually mature family men with proven pastoral gifts. They study in the town where they serve and, in many cases, are able to support themselves and their families through secular employment. The student applies what he is learning as he learns it since the curriculum, including Bible, doctrine, and pastoral studies, is directly related to his on-going service.

Three essential components are involved in TEE.
* weekly meeting at a local center
* self-study materials
* periodic central meetings of the study group to preserve a sense of community

The weekly meeting is a seminar in which the teacher tutors the student, stimulates him, evaluates the work done, and helps him apply what he is learning. The session is personal and student-centered, conducive to developing a strong bond between student and teacher. Often the one-to-three-hour session begins with a quiz to encourage factual learning and concludes with an introduction to the next lesson and an assignment.

Programmed instruction texts are ideal for self-study, but production of them has been slow. Most extension programs rely on workbooks keyed to the Bible or special textbooks. Assignments with questions or directives guide the student in reading, articulating, and applying the materials. During the week, the student must spend five hours on each course.

It has proven helpful for all students from a region to meet together at least once a quarter. This time of fellowship, discussion, prayer, and examinations provides, at least in part, some of the peculiar benefits of resident study which those who work alone would otherwise lack. Therefore, such sessions motivate and encourage students. Annual graduation ceremonies provide additional incentive and promote a sense of achievement.[8]

The impact of TEE is illustrated by a mission in Honduras. By the late 1960s, after fifteen years of work, it had established only two congregations with a total of 35 members. A new missionary began to baptize believers on profession of faith, organize them into small groups, and ask them to select their leaders on the basis of the standards outlined in the Pastoral Epistles. Those selected were ordained and given the responsibility of leading weekly services. While continuing in their employment, they trained in TEE programs. Between 1967 and 1971, twenty-two new congregations were established and church membership grew from 35 to 600. By 1981 the number of congregations had grown to 80.

In an incredibly short time, TEE has spread to almost every country in the world where there are strong churches. By 1982 21,000 students in Africa, 20,500 in Latin America, and another 20,000 in other countries were enrolled. Altogether TEE involved over 360 programs in at least 80 countries, an increase of over 50% during the pervious three years.

TEE developed as an answer to an urgent local need and became a highly effective solution to a common, worldwide problem.[10] When TEE was first introduced, many feared it would replace the resident training institution. In practice, the latter has become increasingly more important in providing advanced training. Resident Bible colleges and seminaries also provide administrative bases for research materials, for writing texts, and for setting up and evaluating extension programs. Often faculty members are also involved in extension teaching.

Other strategies

New approaches to evangelizing are being developed. Many continue making a strong contribution, such as the Rosario Plan prepared in 1976 for the Luis Palau Crusade in Argentina. Some fifty "silo churches" were begun throughout unreached areas by banding together three or four families of believers in a neighborhood who normally attended a church some distance away. These groups were obviously too small to be viable churches, but they provided the nucleus for new churches when people from the area were saved during the crusades. In effect, the "silos" were prepared before the "harvest." Instead of seeking churches to which converts could be sent after the crusade, the churches had already been planned and started near where the converts lived.

Using a Christian family to reach an unsaved family with the gospel is another development in evangelism. The 1977 Association of Evangelicals of Africa and Madagascar triennial meeting theme was the Christian home. Many of the 300 delegates from all over Africa returned with the conviction that God could use the families in their churches to reach families in their neighborhoods for Christ. In Durban, South Africa, for example, Asian families have come to the Christ they saw in the lives of Christian families who hosted them.

By applying anthropology to missions, there is much potential for winning groups of related people to Christ through household evangelism. While each member of a family or clan must believe on the Lord Jesus Christ individually, strategists have found that when the gospel is explained to a whole group with the encouragement of the leader, many more are willing to make a decision for Christ. Such multiple decisions within an affinity group result in a strong unit of believers. Further, the importance of the family as the basic social unit ordained by God is emphasized and a stronger witness in the community is created.

Applied technology

Technology, as well as various evangelism strategies, is important in furthering the cause of Christ. Vastly improved *air travel* since World War II has added a new dimension to missions. Career missionaries can travel to almost any part of the world in a day. Young people and adults of all ages can provide significant contributions to field work for short periods of time, even for a summer. Some missions arrange charter flights to accommodate summer workers and missionaries who take a short furlough when children are not in school. In addition, many national church leaders and students travel to Western countries for part of their education. The result is not only increased convenience, but more important, increased awareness of other people and their cultures, especially by Christian travelers who are not missionaries.

In the field of electronics, technology has greatly affected mission operations. Beginning in 1931 with HCJB in Quito, Ecuador, Christian shortwave *radio stations* have appeared at strategic intervals so that now gospel broadcasts penetrate virtually every part of the world. A recent study indicated that in 1985 Christian broadcasting reached 23 percent of the entire world once a month or more, which means an average of 37 million different people each day.[11] Trans World Radio, for instance, with transmitters in the Netherlands Antilles, Swaziland, Monte Carlo, and Guam broadcasts in many languages, including those of communist countries. Research in 1978 verified that Chinese language gospel broadcasting by the Far East Broadcasting Company is heard clearly in China for nineteen hours a day both on standard and shortwave bands. Transmitters for ELWA of Sudan Interior Mission in Liberia and Trans World Radio in Monte Carlo reach into the Muslim world. Yet, without the battery-operated transistor radio, this massive broadcasting would have little meaning. The development of inexpensive shortwave and standard band radio sets for mass sale has placed a receiver in virtually every home or village around the world.

Many African countries, such as Zambia and Kenya, permit no private radio stations but offer free air time for religious broadcasting on government stations. In 1974 the monopoly of state-controlled radio ended in Italy. Now over two thousand commercial FM stations are in operation, including over thirty Christian stations.

The potential for *television* in evangelism was demonstrated by national prime-time coverage given in several Latin American countries to evangelist Luis Palau's crusades in the mid-seventies. A call-in question time brought thousands of inquiries and led to many conversions.

Of less obvious but significant impact are the *small media*.[12] These include such increasingly available items as cassette tapes/recorders, slides, overhead transparencies, and films. Many mission hospitals now play tapes of music with brief messages in a local language for their patients. Gospel films and filmstrips shown in rural areas by mobile units are also proving very effective. During 1985, Christian movies were being shown to audiences averaging a million a night.[13]

Summary

God provides new strategies for a new age. Saturation evangelism, church growth principles, and TEE have become three of the most influential forces in missions today. Not only did they meet specific needs in the '60s, they continue to increase in impact and significance. Concepts of total mobilization for evangelism, measuring and planning church growth, and decentralizing Bible training have become integral parts of missions worldwide today. In view of recent mission-church mergers, technological advances, and population growth, these developments are especially important.

The application of technological advances has contributed much to missions today. Yet, the greatest breakthroughs involve people—whole congregations of God's people willing to get involved and be used. God will undoubtedly lead His church into further strategies to meet future needs, but the basic dynamic continues to be the Holy Spirit working through believers.

Notes

1. J. D. Douglas, ed., *Let the Earth Hear His Voice,* p. 181.
2. George W. Peters, *Saturation Evangelism,* pp. 27, 28.
3. Peters, p. 40.
4. Peters, pp. 39-43.
5. See David J. Hesselgrave, *Theology and Missions,* pp. 173-223, 333, 334.
6. For an excellent evaluation from a biblical perspective, see J. Robertson McQuilkin, *Measuring the Church Growth Movement.*
7. See *Africa Pulse,* vol. V, no. 3, October 1974; *Latin America Pulse,* vol. XI, no. 1, January 1976; *Asia Pulse,* vol. VIII, no. 2, April 1977; *Latin America Pulse*, vol. XII, no. 4, November 1977.
8. See Kenneth Mulholland, *Adventures in Training the Ministry,* pp. 60-70.
9. Wayne C. Weld, *The World Directory of Theological Education by Extension* (1980 Supplement).
10. See William J. Kornfield, "The Challenge to Make Extension Education Culturally Relevant," *Evangelical Missions Quarterly,* vol. 12, no. 1, January 1976, p. 13; Kenneth Mulholland, p. 112.
11. David B. Barrett. "Annual Statistical Table on Global Mission: 1986," *International Bulletin of Missionary Research,* Vol. 10, no. 1, January, 1986, p. 22
12. See Richard J. Senzig, "Small Media for a Big Impact," *Evangelical Missions Quarterly,* vol. 13, no. 4, October 1977, p. 219.
13. Barrett, p. 22.

For review

1. What are the four basic elements of saturation evangelism? Show how they are related to Scripture.
2. Are the five basic ideas of the church growth movement scriptural? Discuss each as it relates to Scripture.
3. What are some advantages of TEE? How could this approach be used where you live?
4. How has applied technology influenced missions today?

For additional reading

Lawson, E. LeRoy and Yamamori, Tetsunao. *Introducing Church Growth.* Cincinnati: Standard Publishing, 1975.

10

Changes and Challenges in Contemporary Missions

As the missionary enterprise plunges through waves of opposition, the course remains the same but periodic changes of direction are required. The same Holy Spirit who piloted the early church through unchartered seas is guiding church and mission leaders today into new resources, new perspectives, and new approaches.

New sources of personnel

Our world changes faster and more profoundly with every passing decade. At the same time, the need, opportunity, and means for evangelizing the world are increasing.

Third World missions

Third World refers to those nations not aligned with the communist bloc headed by Russia or the capitalist bloc headed by the United States. Following World War II, most churches established by Western missionaries in Africa, Asia, and Latin America became self-governing and, to a large extent, self-supporting.[1] For many, independence has increased concern to become missionary-sending churches.

This development comes at a time when North American missionaries, serving as two-thirds of the world mission force, are not always welcome or willing to minister overseas. Inflation, rising costs, and a trend toward isolationism in the United States have made increased personnel and financial resources more difficult to find. In this challenging situation, the Holy Spirit is leading believers in Third World countries to cross cultural barriers and take the Word to unreached peoples.

Until recently, many churches around the world seemed to believe that pioneer evangelism was the exclusive work of North American or European missionaries. We have supposed that missions was a straight line, a job which could be started and ended in a given period of time, rather than a circle. "Missions goes full circle when a new church that is planted by the first mission gives birth to a mission of its own."[2]

Among Third World nations, the largest number of missionaries come from churches and mission boards in Nigeria, India, Ghana, and Kenya. While statistics are constantly changing and difficult to obtain, by 1985 at least twenty thousand Protestant missionaries had been sent out and supported by Third World churches. About 90 percent are engaged in evangelism and/or church-planting, a much higher proportion than among those from Western countries.

"The Dani Tribe in West Irian, which received the gospel for the first time in 1957, has sent out over one hundred missionaries to other areas and tribes in a spontaneous missionary movement."[3] While statistics vary, this story is repeated in Japan, Taiwan, Korea, and countries on every continent. By 1980, for instance, the Evangelical Missionary Society of the Evangelical Church of West Africa was supporting 400 missionaries in cross-cultural ministry throughout West Africa with special attention being given to Muslim tribes.

Third World missionaries enjoy some advantages. While there still may be cross-cultural barriers, the unreached areas are closer to them than to North American or European missionaries. They can enter countries that missionaries from Western countries cannot. However, this also may be reversed. Japan accepts Americans but not Koreans. Financial support and adjustment to new cultures are often as great or greater problems for Third World missionaries as for those from Western countries.

The most effective mission work takes place when workers go as a team and converge on an area for evangelism and church planting. While financial considerations may limit the distance they can travel, most Third World believers do not have to go very far to evangelize in another culture.

The growing missions involvement of Third World churches is encouraging, but should not be overestimated when considering the total force needed to evangelize the world. The problem of obtaining sufficient personnel remains since 3 billion people are presently without the gospel and the population continues to increase.

Mission leader Clyde Taylor writes: "We would caution Western missions not to excuse themselves from responsibilities in the Third World, reasoning that the new agencies will take over this huge task . . . we know, as they do, that their endeavor should be evangelism and church planting and not the establishment of expansive institutions. All of us have the responsibility of encouraging, praying for, and helping each other in every way possible. The Great Commission is still valid and impinges on the church in every land."[4]

Short-term service

In the early '60s, long-accepted assumptions that missionary commitment was for life and that people over thirty years of age were too old to be involved were challenged. A new trend in missions recruitment has developed where individuals are assigned to specific projects for a term lasting up to two years.

Following the example of the Peace Corps which provided short terms of service in newly independent nations, hundreds of young teachers and support personnel were recruited. An interest in missionary service and concern that these new countries might soon be closed to all but medical or educational work motivated the involvement of many young adults. Here was an opportunity to test first-hand their potential for missions. It was a time to learn by apprenticeship, to serve, and to gain perspective on their lives and values. At the same time, an increasing number of people began taking early retirement and found their way overseas to a second career in hostels for missionary children, accounting, construction, or other support work. Sometimes parents visited missionary children on the field and stayed on or returned to help.

Summer vacation became an opportunity for thousands of Christian students to minister in another culture. They became involved in such activities as literature distribution, musical ministry, door-to-door witnessing, various types of evangelism, and construction projects for national churches and missions. While summer missions might be briefer than other short-term assignments, many other individuals can be involved. Often fellow students as well as home churches provide the finances needed. Many participating congregations and Christian schools testify to a new or renewed missionary vision as students realize that they have been involved firsthand in communicating the gospel and share this excitement with their peers, parents, and friends.[5]

In short-term mission work, lack of experience and, in some cases, training may restrict the kind and extent of ministry possible. Learning to live and communicate in a new culture while learning to recognize its values takes more time than is usually available. Considering the brief time overseas, travel cost is very high. Such a short involvement also tends to exclude continuity of relationships, a factor of great importance to national believers.

For the greatest benefit, the short-termer needs to be selected carefully, given as much preparation and orientation as possible, and assigned to a field where he is able to meet a real need. Missions and sending churches have made great improvements in the program since its beginning. Now, short-termers can free career missionaries for more specialized work and share their enthusiasm in home churches later. In the process, missions will be enriched and a significant number of short-termers will become long-termers.

The value of short-term service far outweighs its limitations. Interest continues to grow. In 1965, 580 short-termers were working with evangelical missions. By 1980 the number increased to 16,608.[6] Now, about 32 percent of all North American personnel in missions are short-termers with a projection that the number will continue to increase. This is hopeful news since a quarter of these become career missionaries.[7]

Cross-cultural communication issues

As new nations have emerged in the last twenty-five years, the whole non-Western world has come alive with ethnic pride and a greater sense of national identity. In Asia and Africa, a resurgence of ancient religions, such as Shintoism and Animism, tends to reinforce the independence of new nations. Many voices are calling the Bible a white man's book and Christianity a Western religion. They are rejecting its message as culturally irrelevant and potentially offensive to their people.

To communicate the revelation of God in Scripture across cultural barriers, resistance to God's eternal truth must be overcome. Anthropologist Allen R. Tippett says, "The greatest methodological issue faced by the Christian mission in this day is how to carry out the Great Commission in a multi-cultural world, with a gospel that is both truly Christian in content and culturally significant in form."[8]

Contextualization

Contextualization reflects a deep concern of mission personnel to communicate effectively so that they can disciple all nations as commanded in Matthew 28:20. The Greek word for *nations* in this verse is "foreigners," or in today's terminology, "ethnic groups."[9]

Contextualization refers to the understanding, expression, and application of biblical truth in a given culture. It seeks to communicate truth in language and forms which a hearer in another culture can appreciate. Yet, it goes deeper than that. Some have paralleled the word with *indigenization,* which means "growing out of the situation." This would involve making eternal, absolute truth so real in a given culture that it is thought of as normal and completely relevant to that situation.[10] The ultimate example of contextualization is the event of the incarnation when the invisible Jehovah took on human flesh, became a real person, and lived in a real culture at a definite point in time. The Apostle Paul, in turn, committed himself to become all things to all men, not in changing truth, but in expressing and applying it in terms of the receiving culture.

The issue is, in reality, a tension between the absolute truth of Scriptures recorded in Hebrew and Greek word concepts and the expression and application of that truth for and by people in very different cultural settings. Failure to interpret and relate biblical truth correctly results in a mixture of human religion and divine revelation. Missionaries are becoming increasingly aware of the deep need for the power of the Holy Spirit to reveal and relate Bible truths as they seek to communicate them across cultural barriers.

Syncretism

The uniqueness of Christianity is increasingly under attack. Many view Christianity as a religion with human origin which is competing with the other great religions of the world. If all religions have some good in them, as some say, why should Christianity be considered better than others? Why try to change another man's religion, especially when it has ethnic and national roots? If all religions have value, why not combine them with Christianity? This approach of putting together various beliefs is called *syncretism*.

There has always been a tendency to compromise the uniqueness of God with the religions of men. God constantly warned His people against merging with the Canaanite religion. Syncretism is based on the premise that God and His Word are good but not unique and Christian truth can blend with human religious thought and ceremony.

Syncretism also has resulted from a rejection of Western culture as part of Christianity. Probably this accounts for many of the 6,000 African churches outside the traditional denominations who have introduced unbiblical teachings and practices in opposition to traditional Christianity. But Christianity is not a Western religion. While Western culture reflects a long contact with Judaic and Christian influences and many nations first heard the gospel from North American or European missionaries, most biblical characters and events were located in that small territory where Africa, Europe, and Asia meet. Jesus' human roots were not European, Asian, or African. He was a Jew, coming from the lineage and culture of a unique race which began with Abraham.

The danger of syncretism is its departure from the uniqueness of God's means of salvation which alone redeems men. It can best be countered by intensive, widespread teaching of biblical truth as well as communication and application of that truth in ways appropriate to the local culture.

Liberation theology

When Jesus said in Luke 4:18 that He came to "preach the gospel to the poor . . . to proclaim release to the captives . . . to set free those who are downtrodden," did He promise and command His followers to revolutionize society? Originating in Latin America at the beginning of the 1970s, a liberation theology movement set its goal as "liberation from all that limits or keeps man from self-fulfillment."[11] It addresses itself to redemption of the whole man. The whole society is restructured, by force if necessary, to rectify political, social, and economic injustices.

While the objective is desirable, most evangelicals would await its final achievement in the millennial kingdom and are hesitant to try to bring these conditions about today. Further, the statements and conduct of Jesus and His apostles do not support involvement in violence.

Liberation theology tends to obliterate distinctions between the church and the world and define salvation as social, economic, and political freedom.[12] Conversion, with its salvation from the guilt and power of sin, is often made obscure or bypassed. These presuppositions, strategies, and objectives reflect Marxism.

Poverty and oppression are serious issues. However, they cannot be solved by an approach which begins with the problem and then reads into Scripture a message and strategy which it does not really contain.

Churches and missions have probably expressed more compassion and, directly or indirectly, produced more social and physical improvement than any single force apart from government. National disasters, famine, and human needs continue to elicit considerable practical response from Christians. It is important to maintain a biblical perspective and minister by all legitimate means to the whole man.

Translation and linguistics

As missionaries have penetrated unreached areas of the world, they have discovered hundreds of tribes with little or no written language. Cameron Townsend, who arrived in Guatamala in 1917 as a Bible salesman, was one of the first to understand the implications of this language problem. In hopes of dealing with the situation, he opened Camp Wycliffe in 1935 with two students in an abandoned farmhouse. Wycliffe Bible Translators has now grown to a force of about thirty-five hundred workers drawn from twenty-one countries. They are working in over five hundred languages and have translated some or all the Bible, as well as other literature, into most of these languages. With the addition of the Jungle Aviation and Radio Service (JAARS), Wycliffe has made a significant contribution to missions today.

Research and planning

In recent years, the need to evaluate mission work, identify people to be reached, and develop effective strategies has made the whole missions community alert to the value of research.

Since the early '60s, the church growth movement has emphasized the significance of asking why some churches grow and others do not. They are probing for ways to increase the church's impact on the lost world around it and to measure its growth. In the mid-1960s, the International Christian Organization (formerly Intercristo), acting as a link between the potential missionary and the sending agency, began to provide personnel information.

The data bank on unreached peoples in the Missions Advance Research and Communication Center (MARC) computers is the most comprehensive in the world. Established in 1966, MARC provides missions-related information, evangelism research, management training, and consultation. The organization also publishes updates on the progress of missions and evangelism in many countries of the world, aids for the missionary program of local churches, and other missions-oriented materials.

A strong impetus for research in missions came from the International Congress on World Evangelization held at Lausanne, Switzerland, in 1974. Representatives from many countries brought reports of the church in their areas. Growing out of the congress itself, the Lausanne Committee for World Evangelization has undertaken a new phase of research. Its Strategy Working Group of nine individuals has two goals: a complete listing with pertinent information on all unreached peoples of the world and the development of strategy to reach each group.

Bringing together key leaders involved in various phases of evangelism worldwide provides important resources for planning. For example, the June 1980 Consultation on World Evangelization in Pattaya, Thailand assigned 17 task forces to seek "keys to unlock the minds and hearts" of major unreached groups.

Much effective research takes place on the local level. In 1975 a church-appointed task force studied a region in central Nigeria which included some thirty tribal groups. The purpose of the research was four-fold:

> To identify and describe the various unevangelized peoples of central Nigeria, to expose the need of these target groups before the church body of Nigeria, to point out factors that have hindered (or encouraged) evangelism in these groups, and to suggest a strategy that is culturally related and one that will enable the church in Nigeria to grapple realistically with the completion of the task.[13]

Researchers found a receptive group of people and recommended that Nigerian churches immediately send 100 workers to evangelize the area. In response, workers went and lived in household villages, won people to the Lord, and began to plant churches.

How effective is a local church's impact on the community for evangelism? This crucial question is the subject of *What's Gone Wrong With the Harvest?* by James F. Engel and H. Wilbert Norton. The communication principles explained in this research-oriented volume are of great importance to the church and missions worldwide. The spiritual-decision process, which lists on a progressive scale the responses of an individual to spiritual facts, is emphasized. Responses range from a simple awareness of a supreme being without knowledge of the gospel (step one) to repentance and faith in Christ (step eight). From there, the new believer moves on from incorporation into the body of Christ to productive service and witness.

Summary

Today, the world is infinitely complex. God has opened additional sources of mission personnel, particularly short-term workers and believers from Third World churches. More than one hundred fifty independent nations in the world teem with national pride and intense cultural consciousness. In some areas, men are restless under repressive regimes. Such conditions raise a multitude of new issues and challenges for our generation.

Research is needed to understand our world from a missions perspective, to develop misson resources, and to evaluate our strategy for reaching the unreached. The world into which Christ sends His disciples today is a world of changes and challenges resulting from an increasing population and other complexities. It is a world which He intends to evangelize through His people. In the days of David, the tribe of Issachar "had understanding of the times, to know what Israel ought to do" (1 Chron. 12:32, KJV). Today, we need to be people who anticipate what God is doing and willingly involve ourselves in the things He would have us do.

Notes

1. See C. Peter Wagner, *Stop the World I Want to Get On,* pp. 106, 107; *Evangelical Missions Quarterly,* vol. 11, no. 4, October 1975, pp. 256-258.
2. Wagner, p. 103.
3. J. Herbert Kane, *Understanding Christian Missions,* p. 364.
4. *Evangelical Missions Quarterly,* vol. 10, no. 1, January 1974, p. 65.
5. See William R. Pencille, "Summer Missionaries—Are They Worth It?" *Evangelical Missions Quarterly,* vol. 11, no. 4, October 1975, p. 227.
6. Missions Advanced Research and Communications.
7. Edward R. Dayton, ed., *Mission Handbook,* pp. 31, 35.
8. *Evangelical Missions Quarterly,* vol. 14, no. 1, January 1978, p. 13.
9. W. F. Arndt, and F.W. Gingrich, *A Greek English Lexicon of the New Testament,* p. 217.
10. See J.D. Douglas, ed., *Let the Earth Hear His Voice,* pp. 1218-1228; David J. Hesselgrave, *Theology and Missions,* pp. 71-127; *Latin America Pulse,* vol. II, no. 2, February 1976.
11. Gustavo Gutierrez, *A Theology of Liberation,* p. 27.
12. John R. Stott, *Christian Mission in the Modern World,* pp. 92-101.
13. Wade T. Coggins and Edwin L. Frizen, *Evangelical Missions Tomorrow,* p. 58. See *Africa Pulse,* August 1976.

For review

1. In what ways are Third World missions significant? What are their strengths and limitations?
2. What are some advantages and limitations of short-term service?
3. What is meant by contextualization? Why is this such an important concern today?
4. What has contributed to the growing importance of research and planning in missions?

11

Contemporary Opportunities

While most Christians are aware of their responsibility to the lost and are willing to be involved in missions, some wonder whether many opportunities are left for evangelism around the world. Since missions have established churches in most countries, is there really an urgent need for evangelism? Both the need and the opportunity are overwhelming. A brief survey of the world scene reveals at least three-quarters of all countries are open to missionary activity.

Factors influencing opportunities

Most countries permit evangelism, even by expatriates. Those which do not allow professional missionaries to enter are not necessarily closed to the gospel. Several factors must be considered.

- A country open to missionaries from one area may be closed to those from another. With the increasing development of Third World missions, the possibility of eligible personnel entering increases.
- Since churches have been established in almost every part of the world, local believers may have liberty to witness across cultural barriers within their own land even if outsiders do not.
- Christian broadcasts beamed from powerful transmitters can penetrate virtually every part of the world with programming in all the major languages as well as many local dialects. With transistor radios readily available almost everywhere, potential exists for communicating the basic gospel message even where immigration, public assemblies, or witnessing are restricted.
- Professional people, such as businessmen, scientists, engineers, and students, often can enter and reside in countries officially closed to career missionaries. While evangelistic efforts may be strictly limited, these individuals can have a significant personal witness with key nationals.
- The factors which open or close a country to the gospel can change dramatically and unexpectedly. A country long open to the gospel, like Vietnam, suddenly can close while others firmly closed, like the Sudan, can reopen.

- The availability of resident visas for foreign missionaries does not in itself indicate the potential for evangelism in a country. In a land completely open to missionaries and containing many established churches, spiritual deadness, internal conflict in the church, or poor church-mission relationships may leave evangelism fruitless. On the other hand where political pressures, poverty, and other problems prevail, the church may grow in a spectacular way, as it did in Ethiopia in the '30s and the '70s.
- A country may open its doors to missionaries and yet limit their activity to certain sectors of the population. Colombia, Venezuela, and Brazil have been open to Christian missions for many years, yet each has increasingly limited missionary work among tribal Indians.

Survey of opportunities

Compiling a list of the attitudes felt toward missions by all countries at any given time is difficult. Yet, it is helpful to have a general idea of where missionaries may go and to pray concerning where they may be able to go in the future. The information given below categorizes countries with regard to their openness to the gospel. To some extent, this survey refers particularly to the potential for North American personnel because they make up such a large portion of the world missionary force. Also, data is not available on how each country would respond to nationals from Third World churches seeking entrance to evangelize their people.

While some of the situations described will change in the next few years, most are likely to prevail for some time. Mission boards working in particular areas can provide updated information.

Continuing or improving

Greater Europe: Austria, Belgium, Finland, France, Iceland, Ireland, Italy, Netherlands, Norway, Portugal, Spain, Sweden, Switzerland, United Kingdom, West Germany

Asia: China (Taiwan), Japan, Korea, Oceania (island countries), Pakistan, Singapore

Middle East: Jordan, Lebanon

Africa: Botswana, Burundi, Cameroon, Central African Republic, Gabon, Gambia, Ghana, Ivory Coast, Kenya, Liberia, Malawi, Mali, Niger, Nigeria, Republic of South Africa, Rwanda, Senegal, Sierra Leone, Sudan, Swaziland, Tanzania, Togo, Uganda, Upper Volta, Zaire, Zambia, Zimbabwe.

South America: Ecuador, Guyana, Venezuela, Surinam, Peru, Bolivia, Paraguay, Uruguay, Chile, Argentina

Caribbean: Barbados, Dominican Republic, Grenada, Haiti, Jamaica, Trinidad, Tobago, Bahamas, Netherland Antilles, and French Antilles

Central America: Belize, Guatemala, El Salvador, Honduras, Nicaragua, Costa Rica, Panama, Mexico

Decreasing or limited

Europe: Greece, Yugoslavia
Asia: Bangladesh, India, Indonesia, Sri Lanka, Nepal, Thailand
Middle East: Egypt, Israel, Syria, United Arab Emirates, Yemen
Africa: Algeria, Angola, Benin, Chad, Ethiopia, Guinea, Guinea Bissau, Malagasay Republic, Mozambique, Morocco
South America: Colombia, Brazil
Caribbean: None

Seriously restricted or closed

Europe: Albania, Bulgaria, Czechoslovakia, Denmark, East Germany, Hungary, Latvia, Lithuania, Poland, Romania, Union of Soviet Socialist Republics
Asia: Afghanistan, Burma, Kmer Republic (Cambodia), Tibet, Peoples Republic of China, Iran, Iraq, North Korea, Laos, Mangolia, Malaysia, Saudi Arabia, Turkey, Vietnam
Middle East: Kuwait, South Yemen
Africa: Libya, Mauritania, Somali Republic, Tunisia
Caribbean: Cuba

The missionary force

To what extent are Jesus' followers in this generation obeying His command to bear witness to Him to the remotest parts of the earth and to make disciples of all nations? Half the people alive today never have heard of Jesus Christ; most of the other half have no real idea of who He is. North American Protestant missionaries total 54,300, about two-thirds of the world force. Serving in approximately 180 countries, they include 37,300 career personnel and 17,000 short term workers.

Other nations contribute about 19,000 missionaries. The United Kingdom has sent out approximately 5,800 workers while the remainder have come from Austria, Sweden, West Germany, Norway, South Africa, and Switzerland. As early as 1972, 200 Third World mission agencies sent out about 3,000 missionaries, with the total exceeding 20,000 by 1985.

A significant resource for measuring the involvement of North American churches is *Mission Handbook,* published periodically by MARC. A brief profile of mission agencies telling the number of their personnel by countries of service and types of work involvement is given. Another section lists the mission agencies working in each country and statistically shows what their people are doing. Information on mission associations, missionary training institutions, and professors of missions also are provided.

The mission field

In 1980 there were 4.4 billion people in the world.[1] The population is predicted to double by the year 2021. At the present rate, there will be 70 billion people on the earth within 160 years. The slight decrease in the growth rate recently is important because the world could not sustain even half of this projected 70 billion.[2]

Forty-eight percent of the world's population lives in four countries: China, India, the Soviet Union, and the United States. Fifty-seven percent of all people live in Asia. In 1980, 39 percent of the world's people were living in urban areas. By 2000 this is expected to exceed 50 percent. The trend toward urbanization is highly significant for mission strategy, the development of personnel, and the structure of the church.[3]

The gap between rich and poor nations continues to widen. By 1980, many industrial nations achieved an annual per person gross national product of $7,550. In the United States the average was $9,000 and in Canada $8,000. In contrast, the poor nations of the world, with over 1.5 billion people, have an average of about $200 per person.[4] The majority of people in Asia, Africa, and Latin America live marginally and miserably. The United Nations Food and Agriculture Organization estimates that over 460 million people are severely undernourished. Another billion suffer from varying degrees of malnutrition. At least ten thousand people die daily from hunger-related causes. Researcher Needham summarizes the situation: "The conditions of life for at least 40 percent of the people in the less developed nations can be briefly stated: life is short—disease is widespread—poverty is general—opportunities for improvement are limited—freedom is for the few."[5]

Western nations have by far the greatest financial potential for missions involvement. Resources in much of the rest of the world, where the greatest mass of the unreached live, are very limited. The payment of pastors and other vocational Christian workers, the building and staffing of training schools for church leaders, the production of literature, the support of missionaries, and the construction of church buildings would be very meager if it were not supplemented.

As with the poor and the slaves of the Roman Empire in the first century, the very hopelessness and helplessness of people can open their hearts to the only good news they may ever hear. Where people lack the basics for living, technical assistance programs can make a tremendous contribution, especially as they are coordinated with evangelism and provide resources for believers to bear more effective testimony to their faith.

Even with our present resources, strategy, and dedication, we are failing to reach most people before they reach their eternal destiny. Jesus' response in Matthew 9:36 must be our standard: "And seeing the multitudes, He felt compassion for them, because they were distressed and downcast like sheep without a shepherd." Serious, consistent commit-

ment to obey His command found in subsequent verses is the first step
we can take to meet this vast need: "Then He said to His disciples, 'The
harvest is plentiful, but the workers are few. Therefore beseech the Lord
of the harvest to send our workers into His harvest'."

Discovering the unreached

In recent years considerable attention has been focused on locating
groups of people who have never heard the gospel. While some believers
live in nearly every country of the world, their impact varies greatly. In
areas such as Brazil, the church is strong and growing; in others, such as
Turkey, it is almost nonexistent. What, then, constitutes an unreached
people? When can we conclude that a nation or people has been reached
with the gospel?

A people group has been defined by the Lausanne Strategy Working
Group as a significantly large sociological grouping of individuals who
perceive themselves to have a common affinity for one another. From the
viewpoint of evangelization, this is the largest possible group within
which the gospel can be spread without encountering barriers of understanding or acceptance.

A people group is considered unreached when there is as yet no indigenous community of believing Christians in their society with sufficient
numbers and adequate resources to evangelize the group without outside
cross-cultural assistance. On the other hand, a people is considered
reached when enough believers and resources are present so that the indigenous church is capable of evangelizing the rest of the group with no
outside assistance.

The report "Unreached Peoples" includes verified information which
challenges every believer and every church concerning the potential for
missions:

> Groups that are favorable toward the Christian faith should
> perhaps be given early attention in evangelism so that their
> favorable attitude may allow them to respond. Attitudes are not
> permanent however; a group that is favorable toward Christianity
> today may change in a few years to be unfavorable. . . .
>
> Besides their attitude toward Christianity, many groups were
> estimated to be "open to change." That is, they appear to be ready
> to consider new ideas (and new faiths) that may be presented to
> them in an acceptable manner. Over 120 groups, with a total
> population of about 248,000,000 people, were reported to be open
> to change.[6]

Large religious groups represent great blocks of people whose beliefs
and practices tend to resist Christianity. These include 850 million Muslims, 650 million Hindus, and 300 million Buddhists. When viewing the
world by countries, twenty-five nations comprising over 31 percent of
the world's people have fewer than 1 percent Christians by the most lib-
eral measurement. "In Africa alone, a study of 860 tribes reveals that

213 were completely or heavily Muslim with virtually no Christian influence, while 236 others were still largely unevangelized, representing 13% of the entire population of Africa."[7]

By 1980 Winter had identified approximately 16,750 cultural and sub-cultural groups. Of these, 11,300 are "hidden people"—those who can be reached only by cross-cultural evangelism. Further studies have described 3,500 of these peoples, noting their location, population, religion, language, literacy, openness to change, receptivity to the gospel, and their level of understanding of the gospel.

Reaching the unreached

The challenge of the increasing millions of unreached people requires high priority planning. Four essential concepts are important in developing strategy to evangelize them.

Endeavor to reach entire groups

Many groups are open to the gospel. When approaching a people with a common bond, value system, and outlook on life, the felt needs of the whole group should be considered as the gospel is communicated. Reception of the gospel by leaders of such an affinity group can prepare the whole group to believe.

Increase missionary force

Since the world population is increasing by 2.2 percent each year, the number of missionaries must increase at the same rate to keep pace with present work. Short-term workers are increasing, but the number of career missionaries is declining. Waldron Scott formerly of the World Evangelical Fellowship says, "Missionaries—that is, disciple makers sent out across cultural frontiers—are needed more than ever. Even Western missionaries are required in many places in greater number than ever, in spite of some voices to the contrary."[9]

While Third World missions has contributed over twenty-thousand missionaries in recent years, many more are needed. North American churches can help by assisting Third World leaders obtain advanced training in missions, Bible, and doctrine either in their own countries or in Western schools which train for church-related service.

Redeploy personnel

As unreached peoples are located and described, some missionaries will have to be transferred from the areas where they have been serving for years. To meet the challenge of reaching the unreached, experienced personnel are needed.

As conditions change or potential opportunities develop, redeployment will also involve assigning personnel to work with hitherto resistant people. While the Hindus, Muslims, and Chinese total more than two billion people, only about 5 percent of the Protestant missionary force is in touch with them. The other 95 percent in Asia and Africa are involved with only 17 percent of the unreached people in these continents. As has been illustrated by the outreach of African missionaries to Muslims south of the Sahara, Third World missionaries can make great contributions in this area.

Make disciples

Churches in all parts of the world must take seriously our Lord's command to disciple. Merely adding converts to churches is not enough. A massive multiplication of workers who go beyond the church, cross over cultural barriers, and make new converts and congregations is the basic answer to the problem of reaching the almost incomprehensible number of unreached in this generation.

Summary

Reaching unreached peoples is the purpose of missions. Biblical doctrine indicates that those still ignorant of the gospel have no hope of eternal life.

Innovations in mission strategy, especially those which involve the whole church in worldwide evangelization, must be developed and adapted as missionaries continue to penetrate and permeate a fast-changing world. We need to look back for assurance, understanding, and perspective. We also need to look ahead and anticipate future opportunities and resources. The most important task will be maintaining biblical priorities in missions. The goals, methods, and qualifications of missionaries always need to conform to the biblical pattern.

Believers living today have opportunity to see the greatest level of worldwide evangelization since the days immediately following Pentecost, but this will not just happen. A sense of eternal values has to control the believer's priorities, life-style, and personal commitment to missions if future generations are to have opportunity to respond to the gospel of Jesus Christ.

Notes

1. "1980 World Population Data Sheet" (Washington, D.C.: Population Reference Bureau, 1980).
2. William L. Needham, *Christianity in the Future; Its Status and Future*, p. 11.
3. "1980 World Population Data Sheet" (Washington, D.C.: Population Reference Bureau, 1980).
4. *World Bank Atlas* (Washington, D.C.: International Bank for Reconstruction and Development, 1980).

5. William L. Needham, p. 11.

6. "Unreached Peoples" (Monrovia, CA: MARC, 1974), p. 21.

7. David B. Barrett et al., "Frontier Situation for Evangelization in Africa, 1972, a Survey Report," *The Gospel and Frontier Peoples,* R. Pierce Beaver, ed. (Pasadena: William Carey Library, 1973.)

8. Edward R. Dayton and C. Peter Wagner, *Unreached Peoples '79, '80, '81* and Edward R. Dayton and Dr. Samuel Wilson, *Unreached Peoples '82.* (Elgin, IL: David C. Cook Publishing Co., 1979, 1980, 1981, 1982).

9. J.D. Douglas, ed. *Let the Earth Hear His Voice,* p. 20.

For review

1. What factors should be considered when deciding whether a country is closed or open to the gospel?
2. What is meant by an unreached people?
3. Explain four basic principles involved in communicating the gospel effectively to unreached peoples.

For additional reading

Wilson, J. Christy *Today's Tentmakers.* Wheaton IL: Tyndale House Publishers, 1979.

Wilson, Sam and Aeschliman, Gordon. *The Hidden Half.* Monrovia, CA: MARC, 1984.

12

Changing Missionary Direction

Jesus concluded His commission to disciple all nations with the assurance, "Lo, I am with you always, even to the end of the age." Until He comes, missions is our mandate. What will the missionary enterprise be like a few years from now? How can we prepare for it?

We have noted the acceleration of change in areas such as church/mission relationships as well as new concepts like saturation evangelism, church growth principles, TEE, modern technology, and Third World missions. We have every reason to expect that God will continue to open new doors, show new resources, and stimulate new ideas as we co-labor with Him.

Therefore, we must expand our vision of what God will do and project plans that will take advantage of the opportunities He gives. Specifically, we need to set priorities for evangelism, prepare new personnel, and project adequate financial policies.

Opportunities for evangelism

Those who have not traveled outside their own country seldom realize how much the rest of the world moves about to conduct business, to study, or even to find a better place to live. Many people who could not be reached with the gospel in their home countries are more approachable when living in a land where they have already had to change some of their customs and attitudes. In addition, political and economic developments have opened areas like Spain and Italy which long have been resistant to the gospel.

Temporary residents

Large numbers of unreached people, such as *businessmen and tourists,* are arriving in countries which for years have been sending or trying to send missionaries to them. Usually these are people of means and influence. Often there is much greater openness when they are in a new setting than when living with their peers at home. People from unreached countries are coming to countries where the church is not restricted and where, by the use of the media and other means, believers have freedom to communicate their faith.

The *international student* away from his homeland is conditioned to learn in a host country because he is there for an education. He can be approached with the gospel in a way that is not possible in his homeland. Christian families can show the reality of Jesus Christ and His salvation in their homes. In effect, they can communicate cross-culturally without crossing an ocean. Also, Christian students can interact as peers. The potential for this kind of contact is much greater than most realize. In 1978, for example, ten thousand students from Saudi Arabia alone were studying in the United States.

Migrant workers offer another high potential for evangelism. Away from home, they are more likely to respond to Christian friendship and concern and listen to the gospel. Turkey, for instance, is closed to public evangelism, but hundreds of thousands of Turkish workers and their families have moved to Germany and other parts of western Europe for employment.

Urban residents

Evangelism in urban areas must be a high priority for two reasons. First, many people are moving to cities so the urban population in developing countries is doubling every fifteen years. Second, people are more open to the gospel in cities than in their home villages, especially when they first arrive.

Roger S. Greenway, an authority on urban evangelism, mentions some reasons why the urban evangelism approach has such potential.

New urbanites are free from the social ties and village pressures which previously kept them from reading the Bible and attending Christian services. In the city they are free to think new thoughts and investigate new religious experiences. During their initial period in the city they are particularly receptive to spiritual truth and the opportunity for personal fellowship. That is the time when they must be reached with the Gospel . . . .

As relatives move back and forth between city and country, the faith which they have heard in the city travels back home. Countless village churches have been started in precisely this way.[1]

In most cases, urban evangelism creates house churches of new believers which result in a whole sequence of growth and further evangelism. Such experiences parallel Paul's in Thessalonica, Ephesus, and other cities.

Of the twenty-five fastest growing cities in the world, twelve are in Asia. Peters comments, "The vast concrete jungles of the cities of the Orient will soon constitute a world by themselves. For me, they become one of the greatest challenges that missions is facing in our generation."[2]

Newly accessible populations

In recent years the northern shore of the Mediterranean Sea, including Portugal, Spain, Italy, and Yugoslavia increasingly has been open to missions. Missiologist George Peters calls this block of people "one of the most needy and most unreached people of the world."[3] Far more missionaries per capita are serving in Latin America, Africa, Japan, or Indonesia than in Italy, for instance.

Areas assumed to be hostile to evangelism suddenly or gradually can become open to it. Believers need to pray while mission and national church leaders need to probe into any indication of changing conditions. An Argentine evangelist says, "There are many closed doors. But many doors are not as closed as we think they are. I feel we should have a boldness and a faith to move out and do things that the Lord could use to open doors."[4]

Muslims

A high priority concern for the future must be the 850 million Muslims, some in countries which until recently were considered by most to be hopelessly closed to the gospel. Referring to the Chinese, Hindus, and Muslims as "the massive omission," Ralph Winter says, "We are hardly even aiming at the major targets."[5] Only 6.6 percent of all missionaries are focused on the 70 percent of the non-Christian world where these people live.

Not all Muslim countries are truly Muslim. For example, only 35 percent of the Muslims in Indonesia have registered. The remainder apparently are only nominal followers of Islam.

A variety of reasons are evident for giving considerable encouragement to making Islam a primary evangelistic concern: changes in modern Islam, contacts between Muslims and Christians in Western nations, and evidence of effective evangelistic thrusts among many African Muslims by west African churches and radio programs. Churches worldwide must exercise concentrated, believing prayer for those who know so much of Old Testament history but who do not know Jehovah or His Son Jesus Christ.

Emphasis in activities

Developments in the past decade all have a bearing on future strategies for worldwide evangelization.

Church growth emphasis

Latin America's evangelist, Luis Palau, predicts: "Evangelism in the future will be tied to Biblical church growth principles. Planting churches and starting new congregations is the most exciting thing in the world. I love to preach to crowds in a bullring, or on television, but my greatest joy is to see new local churches springing up where there were none."[6]

Church growth principles emphasize the involvement of all believers in evangelism and in the life and growth of the church. National leaders are increasingly involved in leading church growth workshops around the world. Self-evaluation, planning for evangelism, and growth are encouraged. As a result, many new congregations will be born, often in the homes of new believers.

Mission/Third World cooperation

As mission agencies and overseas churches complete more mergers and work closer together, the resulting unified command will integrate missionaries, church leaders, support personnel, and short-term workers in their activities. Wade Coggins notes: "Today's situation calls for missionary personnel to be more closely related to and aligned with the local people where they serve. This includes a close relationship with the existing church, greater depth in understanding of the culture, and the development of deep roots within the nation of ministry."[8]

Mission strategy must be based on the concept of the church as the body of Christ. All parts, including local churches and individuals, are interdependent. This interdependence carries serious implications regarding the mobility of missionaries and the possibility of financing overseas projects, particularly since Third World churches are taking increasing initiative in determining missionary assignments for expatriates. In addition to their help in evangelistic outreach, overseas churches welcome missionaries to expand training programs and assist believers in improving agriculture, technology, building, cattle raising, and those skills which can increase earning power. The emphasis always should be upon training those who will train others.

Pioneer evangelism

Pioneer evangelism is not an obsolete concept. Of the 3 billion to be evangelized, only one in five has a local contact able to share the gospel with him. Winter says, "Nothing must blind us to the immensely important fact that at least four-fifths of the non-Christians in the world today will never have any straightforward opportunity to become Christians unless the Christians themselves go more than halfway in the specialized tasks of cross-cultural evangelism."[8] "Many Christian organizations . . . have rushed to the conclusion that we may now abandon traditional missionary strategy and count on local Christians everywhere to finish the job."[9] Although thousands of churches exist around the world, even if all were active in evangelism, they could not effectively evangelize all the unreached people.

The best church/mission relationships on the fields will not guarantee effective evangelism. No matter what the situation, the church worldwide has a responsibility for all the unreached. J. Robertson McQuilkin asks, "Is the foreigner's role that of ministering to Christians as teacher, pastor, or administrator? If so, his role is normally a diminishing one in a maturing church . . . but what if the role is evangelistic, particularly pioneer evangelism? The original missionary role will never cease to exist until the evangelistic mandate of the church is finished."[10]

In view of the vast task and the relatively small number of witnesses around the world, missions in the future must make pioneer evangelism a high priority within the national church and involve increasing numbers of evangelizing missionaries. To implement this plan Peters suggests, "We must carefully prepare men and women to pioneer such specific assignments . . . . I would like to see mature, experienced missionaries transfer from their well-established work into unreached areas. Relocation of missionaries is not easy but it is essential."[11]

Missionary personnel

There is a myth that missionaries are too numerous or not wanted in non-Western countries. Yet, there is only one missionary for every 100 Americans employed overseas in secular positions. Speaking for his people to an American audience, a South American evangelist states: "No matter what anyone says, the ministers and the believers in Latin America want more evangelism—they want more Bible teaching . . . . I would like to encourage you to start new fields—send out more missionaries, with a view of planting churches."[12]

Some strategists are calling for at least 120,000 new missionaries by the year 2000. Since only 5% of missionary personnel are working in new areas, the proportion assigned to "cutting edge" evangelism must also be raised drastically.[13]

Qualifications

Attitudes essential for missionaries in the future include:
- A sense of being securely anchored in the will of God and a confidence that no matter where He leads, God is reliable and never makes a mistake.
- A healthy sense of self-esteem and an appreciation of what God has done and is doing in one's life.
- A secure family relationship, especially in view of the breakdown of the home in many sending countries and the pressures of living in another culture.
- A healthy respect for colleagues and nationals, not judging them by Western criteria.
- A desire to establish close relationships with nationals by learning and serving together.
- A coping strategy for cross-cultural communication through pre-field study and willingness to adjust rather than retreat.
- A servant heart which appreciates differences in peoples' gifts and roles but not in their worth or status.
- A willingness to change and to surrender rigidity for flexibility, especially in cultural matters.
- An awareness of Christ's incarnation as our model for identification with others.

- A feeling of unity with Christ's body and a desire to identify with believers nearby.[14]

Supplemental sources

Many *young adults* are coming to know Christ on secular college campuses. Their enthusiasm over a new life in Christ often results in commitment to missions. In most cases, their educational experience has made them more tolerant of other people, especially those from other ethnic and cultural groups.

Retirees bring perspective, skills, and rich experience to missions. Often they are able to support themselves when taking short assignments for which they are particularly qualified.

Worldwide business assignments continue to increase making possible a personalized witness to peers in other countries. Although certain limitations may be involved, Christians active in international commerce can penetrate into places and people not open to traditional missionary work. At least one organization specializes in recruiting and orienting personnel for this kind of witness.[15]

Preparation

New missionaries need to learn to live and serve with other believers in a church context. They can best understand and appreciate the national church overseas when they have had positive church experiences first in their own culture.

A thorough knowledge of Scripture, including basic doctrine and the ability to apply this knowledge to life, is essential. Courses in cultural anthropology and cross-cultural communication should be prerequisites to service.

Continuing education

Unfortunately missionary preparation is often thought of as pre-field, one-time training which equips the missionary for the rest of his life. Other professionals do not share such optimism. Continuing education is required in medicine, business, education, and many other highly qualified pursuits. Missions is no less important.

After being on the field a missionary is more aware of his educational gap. To help keep his knowledge and work skills current and to excel, he will need opportunities to continue learning, formally and informally, both on the field and in his home country. Supporting churches, mission boards, and missionary personnel need to make further education a serious consideration in their priorities.

Financial considerations

Current trends point to at least three major considerations for financing missions in the future. Church leaders need to give serious attention to these matters because worldwide evangelization is God's primary concern. The greater the resources, the greater our stewardship responsibility in this undertaking.

Available funds

In spite of inflation, Christians in Western nations tend to have more funds to use at their discretion. They have to decide how to invest this money. Missions leaders, pastors, and mission committees bear a heavy responsibility for providing well-researched guidance to help believers make sound missions investments.

Many Christians have considerably more resources available than their missionary investments would sometimes indicate. More believers need to make new, sacrificial commitments for the high priority of reaching the unreached.

Increasing costs

From 1976-1980 unfavorable exchange rates, inflation, and rising costs forced 30 to 50 percent increases in the support levels of most North American missionaries. Travel, housing, education, and other basic expenses increased more in this period than any whole decade previously and the trend continues.

While it is true that in recent years the rate of inflation has slowed, the high cost of maintaining the present missionary force makes it more difficult to add personnel to meet new opportunities. Churches need to consider carefully such factors as the candidate's objectives, preparation, gifts, experience, potential for service, size of family, and similar factors, weighing these against the task to be undertaken.

Third World support

North American churches readily have supported their personnel and projects, but have shown reluctance to invest freely in overseas pastors, church buildings, and other projects under national church administration. With mission-church mergers increasing and many Western missionaries being redeployed, sending churches will have to examine their policies for financing indigenous work. The concept of local support for overseas churches is important, especially when unbelievers might accuse a receiving church with being under foreign control because of the financial investment. But should one part of the body of Christ not help another which has a need?

Dr. Peters sums up the question: "We need to prayerfully consider assistance to churches and missions in the Third World and help them develop their missionary resources. They need and desire to advance in evangelism and missions beyond their present abilities . . . . There is manpower in this world that can be tapped. Can we find a basis on which we can operate together?"[16]

Summary

Missions is the church's mandate until Jesus Christ returns. Whether this event occurs today, tomorrow, or many years hence, we can be sure that Christ will build His church and He will do it through people. All indications point to increasing needs for personnel, resources, and effectiveness in reaching an exploding world population.

Churches worldwide must consider this both their greatest responsibility and greatest opportunity today. Unreached people groups are being located, identified, and described so that strategies to approach them effectively can be developed. It remains for churches all over the world to recruit, train, send out, and support an increasing number of missionaries who will communicate the gospel cross-culturally so that heaven will include "a great multitude...from every nation and all tribes and peoples and tongues" (Rev. 7:9). This number will be determined in part by how many believers become involved in missions today.

Notes

1. J. D. Douglas, ed., *Let the Earth Hear His Voice,* p. 918.
2. Wade T. Coggins and Edwin L. Frizen, eds., *Evangelical Missions Tomorrow,* p. 148.
3. Coggins and Frizen, p. 147.
4. Coggins and Frizen, p. 177.
5. Coggins and Frizen, pp. 22, 23.
6. Coggins and Frizen, p 178.
7. Coggins and Frizen, p. 51.
8. Douglas, p. 225.
9. Douglas, p. 213.
10. C. Peter Wagner, ed., *Church/Mission Tensions Today,* p. 46.
11. Coggins and Frizen, p. 154.
12. Coggins and Frizen, p. 178.
13. Gerald O. Swank, "The Next Great Advance in Missions," *Evangelical Mission Quarterly, Vol 15, No. 4,* October, 1979, Page 206.
14. Coggins and Frizen, pp. 108-112.
15. W. Shabaz Associates Inc., 16580 Eastland, Roseville, MI 48066. See also J. Christy Wilson, *Today's Tentmakers.*
16. Coggins and Frizen, pp. 154, 155.

For review

1. What groups of people should be high priorities for evangelism? Why?
2. Why will church growth principles be particularly important for evangelism in the future?
3. What circumstances will continue to make pioneer evangelism important?
4. Describe the qualifications of an effective missionary.
5. How can your church respond effectively to the financial pressures on missions?

Glossary

antediluvians—the people who lived before the Flood of Genesis 6-8

affinity group—a group of individuals who share common interests

apostles—early church leaders with special authority and qualifications, such as those who had seen the risen Lord; sometimes used in reference to messengers of New Testament churches

church growth—a movement concerned with multiplication of converts and congregations

contextualization—understanding and communicating biblical truth in such a manner that the hearer perceives it to be relevant to his culture

cross-cultural communication—the way people of one society convey ideas to those of another society who differ in such areas as language, values, thought forms, and behavior

deputation—the activity/ministry of a missionary or missionary appointee through which he establishes a relationship with sending churches and individuals for prayer and financial support

discipling—building up believers and training them to witness to others

evangelism—communicating to others the good news of salvation through Jesus Christ

expatriate—a person who lives in a country not his own

faith mission—a mission board which is not related to a denomination, receiving its personnel and support from denominational and/or unaffiliated groups

furlough—a period during which the missionary returns to his sending country to gain new perspective, improve skills, and renew contact with supporters

fusion—the merging of a national church with the mission which established it, resulting in the autonomy and authority of the church over the ministry of both in the area

holistic—emphasizing the needs of the whole man

indigenous church—a church which reflects the culture in which it is located, administering and supporting its own life and outreach

Islam—the religious faith of Muslims based on the belief that Allah is the sole deity and Muhammed is his prophet

liberation theology—a movement, claiming a biblical basis, which seeks to free men from oppressive economic and social structures

missionary—a supported worker who is involved in the expansion of the church in a culture other than his own

missions—the activities of a sending church through which it seeks to communicate the gospel across cultural boundaries with a view to establishing churches that will evangelize

Muslim—a follower of the Islam religion

nationalism—the sense of unity and identity expressed by the inhabitants of a given country

nationals—individuals residing in the country to which they owe allegiance

orphanism—a situation which occurs when a mission disassociates itself from the churches which it has established to the detriment of the people involved

paternalism—a situation in which a mission continues an authority role which inhibits the maturing of the church it has established

parallelism—the relationship between a mission and churches on the field in which each maintains a separate organization but both work together as equal partners

pioneer evangelism—taking the gospel to areas which have not been evangelized

presence evangelism—demonstrating Christianity through a life witness without verbal testimony

proclamation evangelism—verbally communicating the gospel

programmed instruction—self-study books where a correct response is given by the learner before moving on to the next step

redeploy—to transfer experienced personnel from one area to another as needed

saturation evangelism—a strategy which involves mobilizing the whole church to concentrate on making Christ known in a given area

short-termers—those involved in missionary service for two years or less

spiritual-decision process—a rating of responses of an individual to spiritual facts

syncretism—combining different beliefs into one system

Theological Education By Extension (TEE)—individualized training in the Word and church-related skills provided for church leaders where they live and minister

Third World—nations, especially in Africa, Latin America, and Asia, not aligned with communist or capitalist countries

tribalism—a greater loyalty for one's own tribe then for one's country

unreached/unevangelized people—a segment of society with insufficient numbers of Christians and resources to evangelize this community without outside (cross-cultural) assistance.

Bibliography

Arndt, W. F., and Gingrich, F. W. *A Greek English Lexicon of the New Testament.* Chicago: University of Chicago Press, 1957.

Barrett, David B., *World Christian Encyclopedia.* New York: Oxford University Press, 1982.

Bryant, David. *In the Gap: What It Means to Be a World Christian.* Ventura, CA: Regal Books, 1984.

Collins, Marjorie. *A Manual for Missionaries on Furlough.* Pasadena, CA: William Carey Library, 1978.

Dayton, Edward R. and Wilson, Samuel, eds. *The Future of World Evangelization: Unreached Peoples '84.* Monrovia, CA: MARC, 1984.

Engel, James F., and Norton, H. Wilbert. *What's Gone Wrong With the Harvest?* Grand Rapids: Zondervan Pub. House, 1975.

Gerber, Vergil. *Discipling Through Theological Education by Extension.* Chicago: Moody Press, 1980.

Griffiths, Michael. *The Church and World Mission.* Grand Rapids: Zondervan Publishing Co., 1980.

Gutierrez, Gustavo. *A Theology of Liberation: History, Political and Salvation.* Mary Knoll, NY: Orbis Books, 1973.

Hesselgrave, David J. *Theology and Missions.* Grand Rapids: Baker Book House, 1978.

Johnston, Arthur P. *The Battle for World Evangelism.* Wheaton, IL: Tyndale House, 1978

Johnstone, Patrick J. *Operation World.* Waynesboro, GA: STL Books, 1980.

Kane, J. Herbert. *Life and Work on the Mission Field.* Grand Rapids: Baker Book House, 1980.

————.*Understanding Christian Missions.* Rev. ed. Grand Rapids: Baker Book House, 1978.

Mulholland, Kenneth B. *Advertures in Training the Ministry.* Phillipsburg, NJ: Presbyterian and Reformed Pub. Co., 1976.

Needham, William L. *Christianity In the Future: Its Status and Future.* Monrovia, CA: World Vision International, 1978.

Neill, Stephen. *A History of Christian Missions.* New York: Penguin Books, 1964.

Peters, George W. *A Biblical Theology of Missions.* Chicago: Moody Press, 1972.

Stott, John R. W. *Christian Missions in the Modern World.* Downers Grove, IL: InterVarsity Press, 1976.

Winter, Ralph D. and Hawthorne, Stephen C. *Perspectives on the World Christian Movement.* Pasadena, CA: William Carey Library, 1983.

Concerning E.T.T.A.

Since 1930 Evangelical Teacher Training Association has been used of God to strengthen and advance evangelical Christian education. E.T.T.A. pioneered in and has continued to produce Bible-centered, Christ-honoring leadership preparation materials. These are planned to preserve and propagate the rich gospel *message* through good educational *methods.*

Christian education is presented as an important factor in the fulfillment of Christ's commission: "Go ye therefore and make disciples of all nations . . . *teaching* them to observe all that I commanded you" (Matt. 28:19, 20). In order to minister broadly in the advancement of Christian education, E.T.T.A. functions on three educational levels, each of which complements the others.

THE PRELIMINARY CERTIFICATE PROGRAM
Designed for local church and community leadership preparation classes, this program leads to successful teaching for Sunday school teachers and leaders. Six vital and challenging subjects are covered—three on Bible survey and three on Christian education.

Bible Survey These practical Bible survey studies are foundational. They show the marvelous unity of the 66 books of the Bible and help one to grasp the central teaching that binds books, chapters, and verses together.

OLD TESTAMENT SURVEY: LAW AND HISTORY
A study of the books of Genesis through Esther giving an overview of God's working among men from creation through the early days of His chosen people.

OLD TESTAMENT SURVEY: POETRY AND PROPHECY
The thrilling messages of the books of Job through Malachi.

NEW TESTAMENT SURVEY
A skillful weaving of the contents of the New Testament books around the central theme—the person of Christ.

Christian Education These subjects help the reader understand students, teaching methods, and administration of the Sunday school.

UNDERSTANDING PEOPLE
A study giving insight into students' personalities, problems, experiences, interests, and needs.

UNDERSTANDING TEACHING or
TEACHING TECHNIQUES
Alternative texts on teaching methods which show how to communicate biblical truths and apply them to life situations.

UNDERSTANDING SUNDAY SCHOOL
The purpose, organization, and program of the Sunday school.

An award credit card is granted up completion of each course that is taught by an instructor approved by E.T.T.A. The Preliminary Teachers Certificate is granted when the required 6 courses have been completed. A free booklet of information telling how to start E.T.T.A. classes is available.

THE ADVANCED CERTIFICATE PROGRAM

The Advanced Certificate Program gives a deep understanding of God's Word and an insight into the fields of Christian service. It is offered in E.T.T.A.-affiliated Bible institutes* and is profitably presented in local church or community classes. The program consists of a minimum of 12 courses, each 12 lessons in length, and leads to the Advanced Teachers Certificate. It includes the 6 courses of the Preliminary Certificate Program and the following 6 courses.

YOUR BIBLE
An enlightening presentation of the origin and authorship of the Bible, how it was preserved, and how we can answer its critics.

THE TRIUNE GOD
An enlightening study of God, Christ, and the Holy Spirit using nontechnical language.

BIBLICAL BELIEFS
An inspiring study of salvation, inspiration of the Scriptures, the church, angels, and last things.

EVANGELIZE THRU CHRISTIAN EDUCATION
A challenging consideration of principles and techniques for effective soul-winning in the church educational program.

WORLD MISSIONS TODAY
A survey of missions with emphasis on the present worldwide scene.

CHURCH EDUCATIONAL MINISTRIES or VACATION BIBLE SCHOOL
Alternative texts: *Church Educational Ministries,* a survey of the various educational programs possible in the local church; *Vacation Bible School,* a guide for planning, promoting, and conducting a successful vacation Bible school.

THE HIGHER EDUCATION PROGRAM

This specific preparation includes extensive Bible study as well as a wide selection of courses in Christian education and related subjects. It is offered only in institutions of higher education which hold Active membership in E.T.T.A.* A diploma is awarded in recognition of required educational attainment and qualifies the holder to conduct the E.T.T.A. leadership preparation program in church or community classes.

*A list of member schools is available on request.